D0944347

Under Whatever Sky

Other Books by Irwin Edman

Under Whatever Sky

BY

IRWIN EDMAN

New York: The Viking Press

1951

COPYRIGHT 1945, 1946, 1947, 1948, 1949, 1950, 1951
BY IRWIN EDMAN

PUBLISHED BY THE VIKING PRESS IN OCTOBER 1951

PUBLISHED ON THE SAME DAY IN THE DOMINION
OF CANADA
BY THE MACMILLAN COMPANY OF CANADA LIMITED

Grateful acknowledgment is made to *The American Scholar*
in which these essays originally appeared.

SET IN CALEDONIA AND DEEPDENE ITALIC TYPES
AND PRINTED IN U.S.A. BY THE COLONIAL PRESS INC.

Contents

To

Jeanette and James Gutmann

Under Whatever Sky

Introduction

IT IS a disconcerting habit of those who have published essays in various journals at various times to gather these unrelated literary sorties, to put them between covers, and to call them a book. The author of such a farrago carefully admits that the diverse ruminations here presented in one binding actually appeared at different times and are on a fantastic diversity of themes. But they all add up, he says, to one clear total; constitute one lucid system; they inhabit one world, and exhibit a pervasive temper—even a sovereign and comprehensive idea.

As I have reread, with a care I can expect from no other reader, the minuscule essays here included, I cannot say that they all express one theme, though, not to my own surprise, they do revert often to the same or to closely similar themes.

The essay has practically disappeared from the literary market place. It has been replaced by the article, in which some celebrated author or some momentary celebrity tells just what happened in the last war or, with a great flourish of statistics, what is going to happen in the next one. There are profiles, there are close-ups, there are analyses, there are summaries, there are commentaries. So urgent has the state of the world become that such disquisitions are nearly always solemn. Indeed, if they are lighthearted it is presumed that they cannot be serious.

Seven years ago I began in *The American Scholar* a

quarterly department of my own in which I was encouraged to let my mind and my pen play freely over whatever came into my awareness or my imagination. When it was suggested that these essays be gathered into a book, it first occurred to me that I should classify them under several heads. But I found the heads began to knock against one another and it was hard to keep the categories clear. I have, therefore, determined to let them stand in the order in which I wrote them and in which they periodically appeared. They began, as the reader will observe, at the close of World War Two. They have arrived at the point at which soon we shall or shall not know whether there will be a World War Three. They were written at various times and at various places: sometimes at the dreary height of the Ph.D. season at a university, sometimes in the cheerful pressures of a Christmas vacation, at other times overlooking the beautiful bay of Rio de Janeiro or in the champagne-air and Shangri-La solitude of the Wyoming mountains. They have now and again been written out of gaiety and sometimes as escape out of gloom. There were moments when something quite temporary seemed to suggest to me something quite timeless. There were other occasions when I found myself, perhaps in self-conscious desperation, deciding that even the grimmest prospect, say the end of civilization, needed to be regarded with the wistful urbanity of a smile.

I wish I could pretend that I thought that this seven years' gleaning of themes light and serious constituted an intellectual journal of our era. It would be agreeable to persuade myself that I was a small-sized seismograph of the moral earthquakes of our time. I offer these essays simply as the quite spontaneous soliloquies they were as I wrote them. It would be gratifying to find that they contained highly original observations or constituted a world-shaking revelation. It would be almost as pleasant to find that they disclosed quite unwittingly such a recognizable sense of the pressure and temper of things in our time that almost any reader would say: "Curious! *Just* what I've been thinking."

All Time, All Existence

"Under whatever sky I had been born, since it is the same sky, I should have had the same philosophy." Nothing could better express than this sentence of Santayana's the ambition and the illusion of the philosophic mind, the aspiration to survey the scene of nature and of life with such candor and exactness that the prejudices of time, place, and temperament will vanish and that the thoughts one speaks will be the thoughts of Nature herself. I have no such illusion. I know I speak here and now in the fourth decade of the twentieth century, in the aftermath of a world war in which my country was deeply involved. I write, too, amidst the distractions of New York, and in the society somehow commonly known as academic solitude.

Yet I intend to try, under the above title, to exemplify something of the philosophical ambition to see even contemporary things under the aspect of eternity. For, to vary a line of Swinburne's, I have lived long enough, having seen one thing, that all things recur. Perhaps a sense of recurrence is the special insight allowed as a tragic compensation for the tragedy of our time to those of us whose adult lives have spanned two wars.

The middle-aged educated men and women of this generation are those who were in college or just out of it during the last war. They may be forgiven a sense, not without a tinge of irony or cynicism, that this is where, as at the movies, they came in. With quarrels over

6

spheres of influence, and quarreling ideologies of the right and left, they may feel that this is like 1918—or 1815, or, for that matter, like any peace after any war when, the shooting having stopped, it is not as clear as it seemed during the battle just how much or perhaps just what has been really or permanently settled by the combat. Every person of good will knows what he *hopes* will have been settled: peace not only in our time, but for all time. But a generation that has lived through two wars and read the history of many more may not altogether justly be scolded for watching events with an unpersuaded eye, or for feeling that serenity can come only from seeing events in that light of eternity which is commonly called philosophy.

On Being a Philosopher in New York

There are many things that have been called the enemy of the philosophical temper. These include worldliness, the demands and the impulses of the flesh, the obligations of society or family. I am told by my friends in what we in New York like to call the provinces that city life is the great enemy of philosophy, though I cannot help recalling that it was Socrates who said in the *Phaedrus* that it was men and not stones from whom he learned, and Socrates whose mind and spirit languished outside Athens. I think it is not cities my friends mean so much as New York City—which, they will be quick to point out, is not ancient Athens. I confess having sojourned with alternating pleasures of stimulation and peace in academic communities outside New York: Cambridge, Williamstown, and Hanover; having lived enjoyably for summers in small villages in New York State and Vermont and Wyoming and Devonshire and Provence.

I think I know what my friends mean by calling New York distracting. New York is the place where people read the book reviews instead of the books, where the fashions in culture are brief and epidemic. New York is the abode of what Tolstoy contemptuously calls the cultured crowd, and the market place of counterfeit art. It is the city preoccupied with the momentarily famous, the current composer or author or even anthologist, or the bright playwright of the instant. It is filled with the trade winds of culture, and since much of the talk is set in motion by the entrepreneurs, the publishers, managers, art dealers, etc., "trade winds" is well used. New York is too full even of good and authentic things. There is more good music, more good painting, there are more meetings devoted to more good causes, than any normal mind or spirit can digest. It is possible to get a vicarious sense of accomplishment merely by keeping busy seeing what other people have done—elsewhere.

But in one sense, New York may be said to be the ideal place for a philosopher, although thinking in its purlieus, or trying to do so, is a little like trying to sing in a boiler factory. Where could one be as detached as in New York, at least socially? One is loosely related to a hundred communities, but one is fixed in no one of them. Even good causes in New York have an atmosphere of remote control, of being distant and impersonal.

No mean city—if one may borrow St. Paul's description of Athens to describe New York. But if to be a citizen means to be a conscious member of a community conscious of one's existence, one is a member of no city at all in New York, of no neighborhood, of no group. One is as alone spiritually as if one were in an Arabian wilderness, and sometimes the sense is that of a desperate anonymity. I once heard an Adirondack guide visiting New York for the first time remark at the end of his first day, "I saw ten thousand people today whom I shall never see again." Had he continued to live here, he would have come to be acquainted with hundreds of people he would never really know.

New York, then, is not a bad place in which to cultivate the detachment of the metaphysician. Here, where one fits into no frame of reference, one can imagine all possible worlds. Here, committed to no group and to no localism, one can contemplate all time and all existence. I am not so sure that New York is a good place in which to be a *social* philosopher. What is an habitual New Yorker to know of the ties that bind men in a smaller community, the meaning of community itself?

The Athenian thought of his city as a civilization, because he was a part of it, and he thought his life fulfilled in his civic life. It is hard to think in those terms in a city of seven million people. Not even weekly folksy addresses by a colorful mayor, not even the City Center of Music and Art, quite makes one feel the sentiments Pericles had in mind when addressing Athens in the midst of a great war. Perhaps one *could* write a metaphysics in New York, but hardly a Platonic *Republic*. But then again New York is a vast place full of the improbable, and possibly such a book is being written in this monster city right now.

Aphorisms

One way of creative endeavor is the concoction of a series of epigrams. The notion has been put into my head by two recent experiences which, by a slight forcing of the term, might be called literary. One was the reading in part—or as far as I could get—of a collection of aphorisms, so called, by an author hitherto unknown to me, who sent them to me for my delight and my comment. The other was the reading of a section of Franz Werfel's *Between Heaven and Earth*. The obscurer author at least lived up to something like the dictionary definition of an aphorism: "a pithy comprehensive sentence stating a general notion or truth." Herr Werfel's aphorisms were sometimes two pages long. A great many persons believe that any sentence or paragraph set off by itself and not part of an ordered argument is an aphorism. But no such aphorism is likely to be good or true save as it is the distillation of much experience, insight, and reflection. It is easy enough to manufacture pseudo-aphorisms. I shall do so forthwith:

"There is no truth on the paper when there are lies in the writer's heart."

"The business of life is not the purpose of living."

"The act of creation is a birth certificate in eternity."

"Strong character is three-quarters resistance to change."

I am not sure these sentences mean very much, or anything, or that if they do they are true. But printed

1 1

in large type, on handsome paper with wide margins, signed by a nineteenth-century romantic or an eighteenth-century classical writer, I think they would pass muster. It is not easy to distinguish the concise from the trivial; it is child's play to be compact when one has nothing at all to compress. An air of finality, a moral tone, a balanced sentence, a double imaged on-the-one-hand and on-the-other-hand—and one has a minimum equipment to set up as a maximist. Aphorisms are generally on human nature, and their clipped concision suggests that the familiar half-truths they report are whole truths newly discovered. There are a few writers with a gift for conveying in a sentence the substance of a whole morality or world-view, or for disposing of large pretensions with the edge of wit. But the pleasantest surprise is to come upon an aphorism by a writer not known for winged words or dagger thrusts. Thus it is striking to discover John Dewey saying, "While the saint sits in his ivory tower, the burly sinners rule the world." What a comment on the all-fastidious moralists and aesthetes in the twenty years between the two wars.

The aphorism has a streamlined American cousin, generally known as the wisecrack—a quick, evanescent piece of cracked wisdom or, more often, crackling shrewdness. But possibly the true aphorism has died out for the same reason that new great systems of philosophy no longer appear. The world is too complicated to be audaciously summed up in either a system or a maxim. Only a simpleton or a master can say something summary and simple about a confused world. In earlier times either the world was simpler or there were masters in it. One sighs for the spacious days of the old quarterlies, where one could expatiate in ten thousand words. The true master can in a few words speak volumes. The lesser writer wishes he could have three volumes to spread himself in. The weight of a tome at least suggests profundity.

On the Religion of Foxholes

There are no atheists, we are assured, in foxholes. Lucretius long ago observed, not altogether without satisfaction, that religion grows out of fear and calamity; and he did not value religion any the more highly therefor. It is not quite a compliment to God or religious morality to look for a rebirth of religion in extremity only, or to think that imminent death is sufficient proof of the existence of God, or that war suddenly attests God's wisdom to all mankind.

I suspect what religious leaders are correctly noting is not what they regard themselves as observing. In a time of patent and universal tragedy, matters that in normal times are less patent, though perhaps not less universal, sorrow and suffering, are in the consciousness of millions who ordinarily may get along almost to the last breath without having faced the fatal facts of existence. I think it a crude notion that the chaos and destruction of a war would seem to any reflective mind to be an assurance that God's in his Heaven, all's right with the world. But the issues which human existence always raises are made acute in wartime. In war the hideously wasteful fact of death in youth becomes a daily item of mass news. In war the innocent are slain, brute power is in the ascendant. These are precisely the circumstances in which the questions that have troubled men always in times of crisis once more become crucial.

The conventional religious answers under such circumstances will not do, as they hardly do anyway. But neither do the conventionally irreligious ones. I suspect there has been a great surge of interest in novels of the religious and contemplative type because human beings who normally would never think philosophically find philosophical issues on their doorstep. God, Freedom, and Immortality are clichés to ordinary men in ordinary times. But in a world terrifyingly bleak and discouraging, at a time when freedom is threatened and obligation paramount, when death comes in terrible forms and to the young, these terms have acquired force and poignance. Religion is announced to be the way and the life, either in Christian or in Orientally contemplative forms. But I doubt whether people who wondered about God's justice in peacetime will wonder at it any less in war.

By the same token, people who wondered about the meaninglessness of life, who thought in peace that there was more in human experience than is revealed by economic and psychiatric formulas, feel in wartime even more the inadequacy of Statistics and Formulas. The issues of life and death are dramatized in war. But war does not make glib answers more acceptable. It makes the questions—and the questioners—sharper.

Neo-Sacred Music

I have just received an announcement of a program of American Sacred Music of the Twentieth Century, and I have been wondering why I could not somehow refrain from smiling a little, with both condescension and surprise. Why shouldn't there be sacred music in the twentieth century? Why should one so immediately jump to the conclusion that it is likely not to be very sincere or to be very impressive? One would greet in the same way the announcement, I suppose, of a new Gothic cathedral, or a Greek temple of Today, or Homeric Hymns of the Present Hour. There is no reason why sacred music should not be attempted now, or why it should not flow from the deepest religious feelings, or be—in the musical idiom of our own day—quite profound and moving music. But the suspicion remains that it is not likely to be any of these things. Sacred music? One thinks of Palestrina and of Bach. One fears that the contemporary composer will either repeat the old patterns without conviction or genius, or self-consciously avoid them. There is the suspicion that the music will be a little like the Bible in modern American English, or that it will sound like a contemporary novelist trying to have his characters speak in the language of the King James version.

Sacred music has always in the past grown out of a great communal sense of religion. The composer was a close part of the tradition within which he wrote. I suspect from looking at the programs and recognizing the names that there is a sincere but willful attempt on the part of modern skeptical minds to take a deep breath and express a tradition no longer closely or intimately felt. The sacred becomes a theme for grandeur, an occasion, rare enough in the modern world, for eloquence. It will, I suspect, be neo-sacred music.

I received in the same mail an announcement of the St. Matthew Passion of Bach. I hate to be stuffy about the new, but life is short and Bach is beautiful, and I may perhaps be excused for feeling that there will be nothing on the program of Twentieth Century Sacred Music in America that will have anything approaching in either sheer beauty or sheer poignance the closing pages of the St. Matthew Passion. Not that it wouldn't be wonderful to have some composer utter with ardor and artistry those emotions of mankind that are not specifically twentieth-century. Adoration, jubilation, hope, and grief about the central concerns of life are scarcely dead. They are historically old, but each time they are felt they are new. But sacred music? The music, like the term, is likely to be purely conventional, especially if the note be forced.

Sermons out of Church

A group of us interested or engaged in education were discussing how very secular the public imagination has become. "People don't go to church, but they still like to be preached at," said one educator. He pointed to the homilectic tone of some of the most popular radio commentators, the note of edification in the widely read columns of Walter Lippmann, the vast, highly organized women's club lectures, the popularity of the portentous after-dinner speaker. There is a legend that people fall asleep during sermons. If they do, it is a fact that they seem to like the verbal accompaniment to falling asleep. But the fact is that lecture audiences these days are curiously, almost tensely, attentive if they have any feeling at all that the speaker may have anything like a "message."

What are they waiting for in the sermon in print or from the secular platform? Perhaps for precisely what they no longer get, because they stay away from religious services, or for what they miss when they get there: the note of revelation, the accent of ecstasy, the guiding principle, the significant keystone to their lives. Precisely because there is no believable authority, no single authoritative command, they are looking for prophecies. Voices are sought that will make everything meaningful and make everything clear. We are deluged with facts, but it is principles people are looking for. The facts are chaotic and plethoric and violent; it is ideas, even ideals, that are sought. And what is required is the note of conviction and contagion, of counsel that will turn anarchy into meaning, into order. People like to be scolded, as the popularity of Philip Wylie's *Generation of Vipers* proves. And what was Mr. Willkie's book *One World* but a secular sermon that tried to fire the imagination of millions of readers? He was advising us to be "members one of another," as St. Paul did two thousand years ago. He was giving the moral equivalent of the facts of communication and transportation that have made our world one. It will, he said, be one in disaster unless it becomes one morally. That is what Mr. Willkie's book was about.

All those who write of "one world" are, in a very old religious tradition, really reminding us that the bell is tolling for us all. And so, almost every week now, we are told by the wise anonymous writer of the first page of *The New Yorker*. The best sermons are not necessarily given in churches. Can that be the reason why so many people stay away?

(1945)

Brazil Unvisited

In the interest of intercultural relations, a hideous phrase for a sound enough idea, I am writing these lines before going to Brazil. I shall be trying to express certain American philosophical ideas—in English, I regret to say—to our Portuguese-speaking neighbors. But it is not about my official duties that I write here. The preparations for going, the inoculations, the learning of a new language (one confusingly like Italian and Spanish), the excitement of going abroad for the first time in almost eight years, the sense of going to another continent—all this has prompted the mood that comes to the expectant traveler.

Oddly enough, I have a curious regret bred out of previous travel experience. I know I shall never again be able to retain the image of Brazil unvisited. I have every reason to expect I shall be enchanted. Travel films have made Rio familiar; Brazilian songs and singers and musicians are well-known in the U. S. A. I have known two or three wonderfully informed and cultivated Brazilian writers and philosophers. But Brazil, like any other place unvisited, is a residual image compounded of elements furnished by the images of childhood overhearings and random readings. Brazil is coffee plantations; it is jungles; it is a land without any race problems because intermarriage among whites, Negroes, and Indians is so complete. It is the rhumba and the carioca. It is the beautiful harbor of Rio. It is the tropical jungles of the interior. It is the country in which Stefan Zweig lived in his last years; I once heard him say that it was the most civilized place that he, widely traveled as he was, had ever been in.

Some of these suggestions will be confirmed. But every time one visits another society or civilization one acquires new images, while old cherished, uninformed ones disappear. The soldiers in the Persian Gulf Command found out in that parched land why gardens filled with cool waters are so much cherished in its traditional art. Greece was for me always a temple shining on a hill. The Parthenon was there when I got there. But, even in happier days, the visitor saw a rather scrubby, second-rate-looking modern European town. In my own experience only England, at least in the country and in parts of London, looked like what it should have looked like, and felt like what it should have felt like. But then since nursery days England was part of one's familiar imaginative world.

I don't pretend, like Wordsworth, to prefer Brazil unvisited to Brazil visited. But as knowledge grows, illusions vanish. Or do they? Is it not a sometimes almost fatal human stubbornness to go through life keeping the images with which one begins and refusing to give up the illusions even for the sometimes more interesting truth? There are many philosophers who have begun with an image of the universe which no amount of experience will force them to correct. The map of the world one has imagined has a strong hold over the mind even when the true map assumes very different proportions.

I was going to promise my readers some impressions

of Brazil. But I have traveled before, and I suspect, if I am honest in writing in these pages about what is really playing in my imagination at the time, while I am in Brazil it may not be Brazil I shall be thinking about, but Forty-second Street and Fifth Avenue, or the odd limbo of atmosphere of American college education in wartime, or some things in American life that will come up in odd and fresh proportions because I shall be six thousand miles away and living among people to whom the commonplaces of life in the United States are not even well known enough to be rare.

Worlds Elsewhere

Years ago, sojourning in England, I used to be impressed by the attractive combination of provincialism and cosmopolitanism woven into the very substance of English life. In the smallest village somebody had relatives in Canada, or Burma, or India, or Africa. Walking quietly by a Sussex hedgerow would be a man who had spent half his life in the Argentine or in the Andes or in British Columbia. Now there can be no American village that has not learned to accept as part of the natural order of events letters from the South Pacific, North Africa, India, China, the Aleutians, Iceland. There is no part of the world that is unfamiliar with the stride, accent, and temperament of Americans. The stereotyped American tourist has been forgotten doubtless in the past few years. The rich, paunchy, and self-indulgent tourist on world cruises has been replaced by a type of American the rest of the world scarcely knew.

There was a period, beginning about twenty years ago, when the American young began to be known in Europe, a type of youth now almost an idyllic memory, whose hearts were young and gay and for whom Europe was (how incredible it has come to seem!) an escape. They came over by the hundreds in those halcyon summers before 1929, most of them quite unaware of the Europe which was heading toward today's holocaust. The more serious ones were bemused by the past, the museums, and the churches, the more trivial by the entertaining surface, the cafés and the music festivals, of contemporary Europe. It seemed for a while as if American colleges simply transferred to Europe for the summers. Well, it is an understatement to say that young Americans are again in Europe. They are there now not in thousands but in millions. Many of them in ordinary times would perhaps never have seen Europe, many of them would never have seen the inside of a college. Those who come back will, though without the elaborateness of Henry James's heroes, be aware of worlds elsewhere, and be given pause when thinking about America or Europe and the relations between them. One wonders whether, for that matter, the Orient can ever be quite so remote to a generation which has been there in its youth, or even to an older generation which has been accustomed to seeing letters from the East come daily by air mail to Pella, Iowa, or Arlington, Vermont.

(1945)

Talk of the Devil

I notice that the Devil is getting his due again, or perhaps more than his due. Denis de Rougemont has published a small book called *The Devil's Snare,* in which he blames on the Devil most of the separate and several ills that have been charged by more secular-minded thinkers to vitamin deficiencies, economic maladjustment, international insecurity. M. Rougemont says that the Devil's subtlest wile is to persuade us into denying his existence.

I observe in the usually secular-minded *Nation* that, of all people, the movie critic complains that "evil" has become unfashionable, that nobody believes in it any more. It is notorious that Reinhold Niebuhr thinks the world cannot move toward good until we recognize evil in general in the world and in ourselves. The Devil is not always talked about directly; he is sometimes dialectically masked as a *principle* of evil, but the Devil is beginning to lurk in every discussion, and if one does not look out, he will catch the hindmost secular mind.

In a world so full of specific evils and overwhelming miseries and disorders, it is a great temptation to have a Devil to blame, and I am not surprised that many modern minds are re-discovering him, or wishing they could.

Meanwhile, a great many contemporary thinkers are finding in the Heavenly City blueprints of perfection. Perhaps the sacred music I mentioned earlier in these meditations is more appropriate to this era than I had at first supposed.

Brazil Remembered

A few pages back are some ruminative paragraphs concerning impressions I had of Brazil unvisited, and there are added some moral reflections on the losses suffered when ideal images are corrected by facts—even by interesting ones. I am prompted now not to give a *compte rendu* of three months in Brazil (mostly in Rio de Janeiro), but rather to pursue the general theme of the ideal and the actual, this time provoked to do so by Brazil remembered. I am led to reflect on the curious trick of memory whereby the residual image of a place, a people, a country, is not always or often (and sometimes not at all) in the proportions one is sure it is going to be. I am not speaking of memories years old, but of those only weeks old. The moment one is home, it is almost banal to observe, the remembered place becomes a dream. And the shape of a dream, one does not need a great deal of psychiatry to know, is determined by needs, conflicts, absorptions. The geography of recollection is determined by taste and love.

What odd things one remembers about three months of so naturally beautiful a place as Rio de Janeiro! No one could, of course, forget the clear and lovely light over the wide blue bay, dramatically overlooked by Sugar Loaf Mountain. No one could forget either the Baroque churches, especially the classically lovely one on the Gloria Hill, or the Jardim Pubblico, a semi-tropical relic of a romantic nineteenth-century "English garden," with its pool, its beautiful wrought iron work, and its gnarled overhanging trees. It would be hard not to remember the lights coming up in Rio from the height of Sugar Loaf, or the dreamy old miniature Bermuda which is the island of Paetua.

But equally I seem to remember the long lines, often of a hundred people, patiently waiting for busses, on the tiled pavements; the waiters pouring into the little cups the strong black coffee which Brazilians seem to drink all day long at the cafés; the Negroes seated in elegant restaurants, or black and white children playing quite naturally together, or the crippled Negro with the most saintly expression of kindness sitting all day selling papers at the most crowded corner of the Avenida. Or the sound of polite customers whistling for waiters, as is the custom, or the Franciscan monk showing me over the monastery in old Rio surrounded now by the very modernistic skyscrapers of the past fifteen years, which cut off the view of the Bay. And the Positivist Church (I believe there is only one other still existing in the world—in Paris) where for two deadly hours I heard an exposition of the principles of the master, Auguste Comte, and was prompted to think how far pure reason can be from the making of a religion.

And—of all things to remember so vividly—the old-fashioned open streetcars, like those current in the United States once, associated with early spring and summer excursions. I fear a Brazil remembered is no more accurate than a Brazil imagined. But no Brazil-in-itself is ever to be known, not even when one is there.

Other Latitudes

I suppose I am not the only one in his middle years who has forgotten the excitements, the inconveniences, the pleasures, and the perspectives of travel. Travel! To most of us who were young in the 'twenties, it meant Europe. It meant new languages, new food, new ways, and old places, old museums, old churches. It meant another world to live in, a world of taste and distinction. In fact, in looking back, we (at least those of us who saw Germany and France in the 'twenties) see how much we did not notice of what was going on in the present. We were interested in the traditions of the past and in the writing and the art of the future. It is easy enough to smile back at our own innocences, and to tell us we got very little out of it all, except some fussy trips across the Atlantic, pressed duck at the Tour d'Argent, and *Carmen* and *Louise* at the Opéra, Mozart at Salzburg and later at Glyndebourne, or Shakespeare played in lucid German by Moissi, an Italian, in Berlin. All that is gone, and gone forever. I doubt whether my juniors, who are in Europe now on other business, will be going back as tourists very soon.

All this has been brought into my mind because I have been for the first time in many years in a foreign country. I was not in Brazil on a holiday. I was lecturing at the Foculdade de Filosofia of the University of Brazil on, among other things, the philosophy of my own country. But I was reminded in many ways of how it had felt to

be young in Europe in the 'twenties. For one thing, I had
the half-painful pleasure of learning on the spot a new
language, and of feeling the amused humiliation that
comes from finding that one is helpless in a new tongue.
There were all the old pleasures of seeing a jabberwocky
turn into intelligibility; a throaty blur, a babbling murmur, into a language with a wonderful logic of its own,
and a cadence and a color of its own too, and order even
in its irregular verbs.

There are said to be those who believe one impairs the
purity of one's own tongue by learning the languages of
others. I have heard a colleague argue that only those
who know no other way of discourse write good English.
Perhaps. But I remember also hearing it said that the best
way to learn to write English is to read French. I was not
yet sufficiently fluent in Portuguese to have decided what
it might do for one's English. Its conjugations and its
word endings in general bear so close a relation to Latin
that a wave of nostalgia assailed me for the rigors of high-
school classes. It offers strange modulations upon the
other Romance languages one happens to know. Yet the
similarities and differences become a kind of epitome of
the spirit. The human spirit, too, has its modulations and
nuances, and the bread and wine of human experience
are, though the same in essence always, not quite the
same in discourse or quality. The variations in words of
related languages are a wonderful education in the vari-
eties of feeling in human beings.

Why should one learn, a friend asked, five or six different words for bread or wine? Anyone who has fallen a

victim to the passion for languages knows why. Because the words themselves effect a metamorphosis, and the Deus of the Portuguese and the Dios of Spanish are not simply different syllables. Their tone, their quality, modify the soul of the thought itself. At my age, I told myself, I should be doing something else than acquiring a new vocabulary. At my age, however, I was pleased to discover that the tone and accent of a new language spoken by another people fascinate me as of old. By middle age many things have become banal. Given a new name, they freshen a little.

The Bus Trip in the Sky

Travel by air, as by now a good many people must have found out, sounds more exciting than it actually is. It is really, for the most part, nothing but a bus trip in the sky, distinguished by the fact that both the vibration and the scenery are negligible. It is thrilling at moments only: the sight of the receding earth when one takes off, the approaching terra firma when one loses altitude, and the Jove-like sensation of riding above fleecy white clouds. Otherwise, especially on such a three-day plane trip as I took once to Brazil, it is a ride through vacuity. The real sensation comes from the realization that so dull a trip can really be so magically fast. But it is that very speed that is corrosive of one of the pleasures of travel—the classic sense of distance, the slow, gradual approach to another world. In the old days, by the time one arrived in London or Paris or Rio from New York, one was psychologically prepared.

There are ironies, too, in this modern form of transportation—parody resemblances to the days of coach travel. There are the stops overnight at inns on the way, and the fifteen-minute pauses at airports which might be anywhere save for the slightly differing souvenirs sold in Haiti and French Guiana. One refuels instead of changing horses, and the next stop is thousands of miles, instead of twenty miles, away. But for speed I suspect that the stagecoach passenger had more of a sense of movement than the occupant of a seat in a plane. He saw more surely from one inn to the next than his descendant sees crossing the whole Matto Grosso. It needs no Einstein to demonstrate relativity in speed. It is a curious comment on Progress that two hundred miles an hour can *feel* so slow.

Spiritual Snobs

If one were doing a book of snobs, such as Thackeray once did, it would be necessary, I think (though difficult), to describe the Spiritual Snob, who is now beginning to be in vogue again. The snob of wealth, of position, of blood, is familiar. So is the spiritual snob, though he is sometimes so disguised that he seems really to be on the height on which he fancies himself to be. The transcendental Pharisee I think of is masqueraded as a model of pure and disinterred detachment. He is above all the temptations of the world, beyond all the distractions of time. He is a pure spirit beholding pure essences, for their own sweet sake. From his proud eminence there is no such thing as good and evil in this world; everything is smoothed out in his perspective, which is that of eternity. He can survey even the tragedy of our time with quietude, for he holds that the form of tragedy is always the same; and in any case, in the light of timelessness, there is really no such thing as tragedy at all. The Spiritual Snob of our day has quite a battery of great names to quote. They include, of course, Spinoza, though it is conveniently forgotten that Spinoza was passionately concerned with civil liberties. Those in the spiritual top drawer of our time quote the mystics, though they forget that some of them—like St. Theresa —were very busy and socially active people. They quote Plato on contemplation of the One, forgetting that Plato

33

insisted that the philosopher go into the cave and the market place to test and apply his wisdom.

Were I writing such a book of snobs as I have described, I should like to include the Political Snob, too, who will not brook less than perfection; who will not be spotted by pacts and charters and documents, or traffic with actual political institutions. At the extreme he is, of course, an anarchist, all for a society of free spirits, beyond the gross instrumentalities of government. Today he is a nationalist who will not soil his mind with any imperfect world organization, something for starry-eyed global visionaries.

Then there is, finally, the Snob who looks down on Snobs. That is, perhaps, as far as the theme can logically be explored.

The Post-Postwar World

It is some months since V-J Day, and we may, from all signs, be said to be pretty deep into the Postwar World. For years during the War, the Postwar World was a fine-sounding, vaguely precise ideal to which to refer. All futures, all hopes, all aspirations were to be cashed in at that eventual destination. Well, here it is, here and now. This is it. The discharge buttons are almost as numerous as the uniforms; the beauty contests and the aluminum saucepans and heavy cream are with us again. The Postwar World, however, in one sense has ceased to be. It is no longer there as an ideal limit, a *terminus ad quem*, a point toward which all action and all meaning can be referred. To what post-Postwar World, what roughly calculated limit, can we refer the arrival of world government, of the good society, the good life? In desperation, perhaps, for some fixed point of reference, some of us already are beginning to talk about World War Three. At least there is a definiteness, though a terrible one, about that. Or did we all along in our simple hearts mean by the Postwar World what in other days has always been meant hopefully by Utopia? Now with the atomic bomb, it is Utopia—or Nirvana.

(1945)

On Pride in Being Here and Now

I have been running across condescending references to the 'twenties. The condescension is not toward the once-vaunted flaming youth of the period, but to the ideas current, or allegedly current, at that time: the smug materialism, the easy behaviorism, the narrow psychologism of that paleolithic period. There is nothing quite like the intellectual condescension of one generation toward the ideas of the generation just preceding it. It is, therefore, the young, particularly, who pour scorn upon the notions current at the time of the youth of their fathers. But the middle-aged these days, too, are busy saying *"peccavi"* with respect to the things they believed, or said they believed, when they were striplings.

Sometimes, as one hears the dismissal, impatient or patronizing, of notions dated only by a decade or two, one wonders what is so self-validating anyway about truths whose chief claim to impressiveness is that they are being uttered at this minute. The tone of actuality has a certain convincingness, it must be admitted, as have words written only last month or last week or last night. Still, one would think that anyone with any slight knowledge of history, of the changing winds of doctrine, and of the familiar cycles of opinion, would know better than to be taken in by any seeming ultimacy in some current vocabulary of wisdom. Does it go without saying, for instance, that Aldous Huxley's mysticism is any nearer the truth than his nihilism was in the 'twenties? Perhaps;

but his Hollywood Upanishads have the forensic advantage of being dated today; his more earthbound opinions are twenty-five years old. Does it follow that the shock of war and of the atomic bomb has brought the truth nearer to all mankind?

It is not hard to imagine that about 1965, if there is anybody left alive to express intellectual judgments, some young critic, terribly *au courant,* or some elderly thinker, having seen a later light, will be saying:

One must, of course, realize that the writers and thinkers (not always identical) of the 'thirties or 'forties were not in a position to take a long view, or to speak with composure of the noisy and noisome circumstances under which they tried quietly to think. First a great depression, then for a decade the shifting shadow of a world war, then the Second World War itself, coming to a climax in the unleashing of atomic energies that carried the threat of the possible devastation of all mankind—no wonder there were all manner of flights to all kinds of refuges. There were outbursts of mysticism, of cynicism, of despair.

There was an epidemic, too, of soft caesuras, of all sorts of muddleheadedness, crackpot paths to all magical salvations, spiritual or economic. No wonder, either, that social theory, and philosophy itself, became infected with self-conscious psychologism, with endless discussions of the motives behind motives, the feelings hidden below feelings, the fears of the fear of fear. Looking back now from a much less crowded planet (for since the end of the First Atomic War, the planet is much less populated), we see what a confused, chaotic, hysteric world the intellectuals had come to live in in the dreadful 'thirties, the furious 'forties. Novelists turned to revamping forgotten "miracles" or to preaching philosophies with strange nostrums of mysterious salvations. Sometimes, after a lifetime faithful to rigorous method and exact observation, a scientist would right-about-face to suggest that the solution of social and political ills lay in some mystic inner change, some purple sentiment, a moral presto chango. Philosophers, many of them, made common cause with fancy-sounding psycho-anthropologists. It may be hoped that in this Year of Grace, 1965, when there are so few of us left, we will not relapse into such turbid nonsense. At least we have no housing problem now to addle our heads. We can see from this quiet distance in this spacious emptiness why, in the bloody fanfare of the congested 'forties, a great many queer hysterias smugly passed for thought. In those days it was often not possible from their writings to tell which was the patient and which the psychiatrist. The atomic bomb, it now appears twenty years later, not only has helped to clear the planet; it has helped to clear the air.

(1945)

Young Veterans and Heroes in Sack Suits

Whatever is going to happen to certain words that have always had a touch of the grandiose and the remote? "Heroism," for instance. Intellectually one is aware that the young man before one, covered as he is with a "fruit salad" of decorations, is not only officially but actually a hero. But it is very hard to associate the modest youth, wondering what profession he ought to go into, with the heroes of Homer, or even the heroics of Strauss's *Heldenleben*. What is to become of the old phrases—"the heroic mold," for instance? The hero in a sack suit the day after his discharge, or even in his uniform the day before it, is slight in build, casual in manner, unobtrusive in speech. And he is likely to have a sense of humor, too, which does not seem to have been true of the great figures of the Norse Sagas.

Then, too, the term "veteran" still suggests the grizzled, hardened, toughened survivor of many long years—say, the ten years before Troy. Some of our heroes are the survivors of many campaigns over a good number of years. In the Air Forces, a dean among veterans may actually have reached twenty-five. After all, we perhaps do not need new words. We may have to revise our notion of a veteran, but the heroes of the great tradition have always been young, handsome, modest. Our heroes have patently more generosity and idealism than is always obvious in Ulysses.

(1945)

39

War Without Tears

From long force of habit during the war, many of us are still tuning into news reports with the lurking feeling that something world-shaking may have happened during the preceding hour. Some of the more excitable news reporters haven't cooled down yet, and a subway tie-up is exclaimed with the same intensity that used to greet a major victory a year ago. In war at least, something clearly seems to happen. Is it not the human dilemma that the human race wishes the quietude of peace without the boredom of it?

Perhaps the tensions of conflict can be enjoyed with smaller stakes than lives. I notice an arrangement for a bloodless peacetime war has already been made in England. It is a new magazine for philosophical discussion, with the name *Polemic*. Listed for early publication are articles by some of the best-known philosophical writers in England and some of the most combative ones, among others Bertrand Russell and C. E. M. Joad. *Polemic!* The title gives away an open secret in philosophy: that many professional philosophers are more interested in keeping up the argument than inquiring into the truth. A well-known philosopher was described as "having a morbid fear that somebody might agree with him." If we should know the truth and the truth should make us free, some of us doubtless would relish most the freedom to question whether it was really the truth at all.

◇◇◇

Interval for Contemplation

Leisure breeds contemplation, or is at least the breeding ground for it. What then are the free spaces for leisure in the modern world?

Life, even in universities, is, as William James complained, only a series of interruptions. Even when one is free, one is committed in thought. But there is one time when the will is paralyzed, all action seems remote, everything is at one remove. It is during the stages, early or late, of grippe. Aspirin has quieted the aches and pains, and fever the energies. One is too weary to hold even a book, and one is surfeited even with sleep. I think it may well have been in some early stages of grippe that early man made the first great speculative guesses as to the nature of things. "All is water," said Thales, and I should not be surprised to learn that his eyes were streaming at the moment of this famous ontological utterance.

With outer pressures removed, inner meditation begins. This is the time when, sheltered even from the telephone, internal soliloquy can have its scope. It is not, perhaps, the time for organized thinking. Intuitions begin, hypotheses are dreamily initiated under the influence of aspirin or anhiston. In the lethargy of a low fever, conclusions are not firmly arrived at. Thoughts begin and waver, and taper off. But the themes come back. Nothing immediate matters now, and one lies wondering a little what ultimately matters at all. And the play of

4 1

memory released comes into delightful being, recollection uncensored by the necessities of daily routine. Friends perhaps long-forgotten come into consciousness without the slightest uneasiness at the letters one has long owed them. The committee one would not have missed for worlds now seems distant and trivial, and tea long ago in a garden near Oxford seems credibly vivid and ultimate. One would daydream on in utter if languid peace. But what is this I see before me? Someone with a thermometer and a bottle of aspirin—even, or particularly, during grippe the world is too much with us.

◇◇

Order of the Seasons

It is the time of year when plans are being made for the summer. I find it quite hard to realize that it is the cold season in southern Brazil, and quite uncomfortably chilly on June nights in Argentina. Say what one will, to one brought up in northern latitudes, the seasons are standard; winter in June and summer at Christmas are rather absurd eccentricities of lands below the equator. The rational mind prides itself on its amplitude and its flexibility. It will fall victim to no parochialism of climate or idea. There is thus nothing off center, of course, about the Muslim and his Allah, the Hindu and his Brahma. There is nothing alien to us that is human. There, to our enlightened minds, is one world and one humanity. Of course! But winter in July and New Year's in tropical heat! I cannot help thinking the Australians must feel a little embarrassed to live in a region where seasons, by any reasonable man's calendar, are so palpably absurd.

Philosophy for the Little Ones

"But you should write a book on philosophy that children could read," said the lady who was a member of a child guidance society.

"Philosophy is *not* for children," I replied with considerable firmness. "It transcends their range and their interests. They could not possibly understand the language one would simply have to use."

The lady thought a moment.

"I think you are quite wrong," she said. "I think philosophy is just made for children. Philosophers, like children, get bemused by their own words, especially the long ones. Philosophers, like children, enjoy making up languages of their own, and they often get up among themselves a language nobody else can understand. I think quite young children would enjoy the jabberwocky of philosophy very much."

"Do not confuse," I insisted firmly, "the necessary technical language of philosophy with meaningless jabberwocky. Words are meaningless only to those who do not take the trouble to understand them. Furthermore, you don't mean to tell me that the issues of life and death, of nature and destiny, could be understood by adolescents, or that they would care about them."

"Certainly I do," she said. "In philosophy the elementary and the ultimate, I should have supposed, are very close together. You do not have to be a professor to have long, long thoughts about life and death and destiny.

Moreover, a twelve-year-old child would be more likely than a sophisticated adult to distinguish appearance from reality, and not be taken in by clichés and labels. He would trust his eyes and his ears and his, as yet, uncorrupted mind."

"But the principles of right and wrong—good and evil?" I queried.

"I hadn't supposed," the lady said, "that one must wait till one has a Ph.D. to think about those things, or that one actually does."

"Or metaphysics, and the ultimate traits of all being?" I asked. "Is that child's play . . . is metaphysics kid stuff?"

"Have you never seen a child? Have you never heard a child ask what the world is made of, or who made it, and why?" she demanded. "And who else asks the simple questions about ultimate and about simple things that the adult has long come wearily to take for granted? I don't think you need worry that these questions would interest only the professional philosophers or grown-ups. Most grown-ups are not interested in right and wrong, good and evil. At least, they don't talk about them after they leave college. Have you seen many at a dinner party interested in the general traits of universal being? Or are most professors of the subject really interested in these matters?

"It is not only of the children that I am thinking, but of philosophy itself. Catch the child when he is very young, with a wide-eyed wonder about the world, and philosophy will be his delight. It was Aristotle, I believe, who said that philosophy began in wonder. Well, begin talking about philosophy when wonder is most alive.

"And," she added, "would not an ultimate philosophy have something of the innocence, the unbribed attention of children? Would not a sage have arrived at ultimate simplicities again? Really, you should write a book on philosophy for children. They might be your only unspoiled readers. Think of all the false ideas a philosopher might not have to get out of their heads."

"Mother," the lady's little girl called in, "what are you talking about?"

"Philosophy, darling," her mother said.

"Why?" asked the little girl. The lady looked at me with an air of triumph.

"I Have Long Felt—"

"And what do you think of the election of Reuther to the U.A.W.?" I heard the gentleman ask.

"Well, really, I haven't thought about it at all," replied the candid young non-thinker opposite him.

And I was led to reflect on the number of times, confronted with a sudden question about one of the thousand things a well-bred contemporary is supposed to have some opinion about, I have invented one on the spot, *ad hoc* and *ad lib* and *ad nauseam*. Nor am I alone. I have seldom observed anyone instigated by such an immediate and searching interrogation refuse to give a reply and, often in quite grammatical form, a judgment —on Russia, on the atom bomb, on existentialism, on socialized medicine.

Judging by myself, I suspect I know what happens. It is only civil to answer a question. It seems blunt and rude, as well as mildly shameful, not to have a spontaneous reply concerning the major issues that are troubling mankind or the minor problems that are agitating the local parish. It seems as absurd to say: "I haven't made up my mind," in answer to an inquiry concerning Argentina, as it would to say the same words in reply to the question: "Isn't it a nice day?" And once one begins a reply, the rest is all too fatally easy. One begins not quite knowing what it is one intended to say, or what actual opinions, if any, one does have on the subject that has been broached. The theme gathers momentum in the soliloquizing mind. Within a few moments the odds and ends of anything one has read on the matter begin to come together. The idea develops almost of itself. It is a tune that begins to complicate itself in the mind. And the first thing one knows, there is a flow of sentences; and as they flow, the tone of conviction grows more emphatic.

The more one talks, the more one feels in the internal equilibrium of one's being: "This is deeply what I believe." And more than that. Within two minutes, it becomes quite clear to the speaker that these notions which he has quickly marshaled out of the radio commentaries, the editorials, the brochures he has read in the last year, are opinions of his own—long, deeply, and painfully pondered. They are offered now with the weight of conclusions that have grown out of months of industrious and conscientious study and reflection.

"What do you think of Niebuhr's theology, of the new president of Vassar, of the future of air transportation, of book clubs, of the new women's hats, of Truman's chances in 1948, of the nature of happiness?" At the drop of a hat, or of the handkerchief of the lady who asks the question, I would blush not to have a reply. And like many others, I become so absorbed in developing the music and dialectic of my answer that I have no time to blush at the fatuities the answer may contain.

(1946)

On Other Kinds of Starvation

Men are not starved for bread alone, and there is another homelessness current in the world than that with which the housing problem has made us acutely familiar. It would be a cruel kind of preciousness to pretend that there is anything more urgent than the feeding of the starving all over the globe, or the provision of shelter for those without a place to live. But the facts of physical starvation and of physical homelessness are outward signs of another kind of hunger, another kind of homelessness, that is also widely current in the postwar scene. What else would explain all the turnings toward various religions, and various ersatz religions, that have been endemic during these last years? How else are we to explain the avidity with which new moral doctrines—even thin, confused, or fraudulent ones—are devoured, even by people not normally given to philosophic speculation? There is afoot in the confusion of our time a hunger for spiritual bread, too, and, while stones will not be swallowed in place of it, some quite denatured substitutes of moral nutriment will be eagerly gobbled down.

And the return to religion, celebrated, perhaps precociously, in many regions? Well, there are a good many displaced persons in the spiritual sense, too: the liberals who have lost their faith in progress or intelligence, the fellow travelers who have lost their faith in Communism, the skeptics who have lost a sense of being at home with their own disillusions. Moral nutriment is scarce on earth, and people turn gladly to expectations of manna from Heaven. And with no place to go for an intellectual habitation, some mystic Heaven is sought in which, in imagination, one can relax and call one's self, at long last, safe and sheltered and home.

Dowager

I think one of the reasons people like to see Mrs. S. is the air she conveys—for all her personal simplicity and modesty—of being somehow imperial. There is never any evidence in her words or her manner that she ever counts on her wishes being frustrated or her plans impeded by others or by the general circumstances of the world. In an age when most people are limited by obligations or, even if wealthy, by taxes, she still seems to move, assured and elegant, like a luxury liner—as if the world were still easy and comfortable, and as if one could easily go anywhere, buy anything, or cross any frontier. Merely to see her is to move in imagination in the times in which she used to live, when passports were scarcely heard of, servants were cheap and plentiful, and the income tax a remote socialistic ideal. To talk with her is to be reminded of the days of travel in the grand manner and country life on the grand scale.

During the war, she seemed not to recognize the difficulties (that even she encountered) of living in the spacious fashion to which she was accustomed. And even now, you would scarcely know from her manner and her manner of life that servants are expensive and rare; from her habitation in the country that country life on a lavish scale is disappearing; from her ménage in the city that living quarters are hard to find; or from her dinners that good food (or any) is hard or expensive to get.

It is a comfort, I suppose, to know, in a society so difficult and confused, that Mrs. S., at least, has a generous and assured way of living. Only travel abroad is still impossible for her. But within the wide limits of the Western world, Mrs. S.'s life is untrammeled; and her conviction that this is so is evident in her firm and gracious voice. It is a comfort, albeit a vicarious one—and not too great a one—to see someone so snugly smug in a civilization where few can afford to be.

Bibliotherapy

The brisk little man came into my office and said he wanted to study philosophy because he needed it in his profession. In a small South American country (though he himself is a European), he had been practicing what seemed to be a vague, free-wheeling psychiatry. He had discovered, he told me blandly, that many of his patients could best be cured by prescribing the proper books. Apparently quite by accident he had discovered that certain of the books that were most healing were philosophical books, about which, he said, he had hitherto concerned himself very little. He therefore had come to this country for a year to try to discover what curative volumes were in vogue in the philosophic world. He had decided hereafter to confine himself almost completely to bibliotherapy as a form of healing.

The term, I confess, was quite new to me, but it was not without charm. It suddenly made me realize that perhaps the academic degree of Doctor of Philosophy was less of a quack accolade than I had supposed. For years now, I suddenly realized, I had been practicing bibliotherapy. And I suddenly realized how good an excuse there was for selling books at drugstores, though perhaps they ought to be placed behind the drug counter and not given out without a doctor's explicit prescription.

It chills me now to the marrow as I turn the advertising pages of the Sunday book review and see with how little restriction bibliotherapy is practiced by writers and publishers, and by reviewers, too. "This book," the phrase runs, "is strongly recommended." But for whom? by whom? for what disease of the spirit? These long historical novels, for instance: opiates many of them are truly. But is it fair to allow them to be bought by the strained and the neurotic? They might get into the habit of reading such things always. I will scarcely even mention the serious dangers of the unguarded circulation of detective and mystery stories. The state controls other drugs, while it lets these go freely on sale. And there are among books subtler opiates and stimulants than either historical novels or detective stories: works on metaphysics and morals, for instance.

It would be a fine thing, I am sure, if one could go to one's doctor to have the proper books recommended for one's health. But it is my experience that my own doctor is always asking *me* what to read. I foresee a new type of medical education in which, instead of the usual first-year course in anatomy, there will be classes in the anatomy of criticism, and the last-year students touring the wards will look not at their patients' chests, but at their intelligence quotients and at the books by their bedsides.

Before my visitor left I had decided it might be a very good thing if the medical schools were hardly distinguishable from liberal arts colleges. I smiled a little at my visitor who spoke of bibliotherapy, but the greatest advances in medicine have always been achieved over the stupid opposition of reactionaries. Before my bibliotherapist left, I found myself prescribing some good books for him, and for his future patients.

Age of Specialists

Sometimes it takes nothing more than an announcement among the want ads to start one's mind meditating on some vast tendency of the present age. This is, as has so often been said, an age of specialists. But the word "specialization" conjures up, usually, some technologist in nuclear fission or some expert in a gleamingly modernistic electronics laboratory. Speak of a physicist or a radio technician, and one has an image at once of the life and training, perhaps even the spiritual background, of the man in question. I try to picture to myself the history, the education, and the character of the young man who could successfully claim a position on the basis of being "a specialist in hot fudge, marshmallow, and butterscotch toppings."

I wonder what in his childhood and early youth directed this craftsman to this particular and mellifluous mastery. Was it on some rainy summer afternoon at a boys' camp in the Adirondacks, when all were sitting toasting marshmallows before the fire, that his own ambition was first fired to become a marshmallow-topping expert? Was it at some teen-age party when, suffering from the gooey and inexpert fudge provided by the girls present, he decided to become so expert a fudge-maker that sweet-toothed pioneers would beat a path to his door?

What is the young man like now? He could possibly be some reflective and candid mind who, believing that everything is futile and unimportant in the present

55

chaos, feels no guilt whatever in specializing in what other people call trivial. After all, sweetness is an intrinsic value, and how surely could that be said of some of the values that some of the moralists talk about? And with some sudden shortage of sugar might not a man working in toppings and icings feel that he was a kind of Benvenuto Cellini plying his craft in something as rare as antique silver or spun gold? Or, perhaps, so disorganized is the state of the world that the advertisement remains altogether unanswered—and all expertise in sweetness, among how many other vanished arts, has left the modern world to assembly lines and regimented industry.

Remembrance of Trains Past

Every age is, of course, an age of transition, but often it is very small things that make one aware that one is living toward the end of one chapter and almost at the beginning of a new one. I saw a long statement the other day by a railroad president, rather wistfully deploring the things that the airlines were beginning to say about the railroads. I can imagine that a little over a century ago there were stagecoach owners who were persuading travelers not to be taken in by the seductive advertisements of "the covered cars." The railroad president the other day was reminding the public how comfortable, how steady, how luxurious, and how certain was surface travel in streamlined trains—and how risky, bumpy, and generally crude were the accommodations of air travel. He admitted with reluctant candor that planes were faster than trains, but he said that on mature reflection he could not see one other advantage of travel by air.

There is a certain point at which one realizes definitely that one has passed into an older generation. I found myself reading the railroad president's utterances with sympathy and understanding. It was not so much that I was convinced by what he said as that I suddenly realized that for anyone born over forty years ago a railroad remains the standard furniture of his familiar earth. I think a great many people of my own generation think of the distance between cities of the United States in terms of familiar standard railroad time. I really don't

57

care how quickly a Constellation can fly from St. Louis to New York, for every respectable citizen knows that the railroad time, or God's time, is twenty-four hours. There are, moreover, features of railroad travel that to older people seem the very essence of transportation. The long moaning whistle of an American express train across the countryside has a music and a nostalgia that no roar of any stratoliner can equal.

Yet the railroads themselves have become so metamorphosed that I suppose one might as well abdicate altogether and travel by plane. A quiet Diesel engine is a pallid parody of a steam locomotive, and those of us who remember the real days of railroading almost miss the soot and cinders in the new soft luxuries of the air-conditioned cars. I reluctantly admit that though for years I have ranged myself on the side of everything that looked like a progressive cause, with respect to transportation I am almost tempted to ask time to turn back in its flight. I have probably been conditioned by the fact that one of my earliest early childhood memories is that of the last steam locomotives puffing their way on the now almost forgotten elevated railroads of New York. Ho hum, first thing I know I'll be voting for President McKinley!

The Unsuspected Moralist

There is a curious convention of deference we have established in the modern world. I was reading the essays of Frank Sullivan, collected under the attractive title of *A Rock in Every Snowball*. I read them with a delight which that deft and accomplished writer always produces in me. I realized while I was reading that Mr. Frank Sullivan is classified as a humorist, and that such classification immediately prompts the literal-minded to assume that having thus labeled a writer, one need not take him seriously.

That is what brings me to the theme with which I began. In order to be taken seriously in contemporary discussion, one needs to parade the apparatus of solemnity. I am not the only one, I am sure, who has read some quite ridiculous books in the last few years, volumes whose laughable absurdity was obscured by the fact that they were couched in the most solemn language, and under the usual cataloguing system had to be placed among philosophical and learned works. Plato long ago in *The Laws* reminded us that it was possible to be serious without being solemn, and he wrote *The Laws* in his old age.

In Mr. Sullivan's gay comments on existence (sadder below their gaiety than is at first apparent) I found more sensible moral judgments and a better sense of proportion about contemporary values than in many grandiose tomes devoted to a solemn consideration of the same

grave matters. There are works by certain learned soci-
ologists that are, without their half trying, a good deal
funnier than some of our professional humorists could
manage. There are, on the other hand, works by some
of our humorists, and Mr. Sullivan is one of them, which
have far more serious commentaries to make on contemporary life and morals than many of our most pontifical
moral analyses. We are a great people for telling jokes,
but we have been a little ashamed of noting seriously
what our humorists are driving at. That is why it is now
only very lately being adequately realized how very
much more than a joker Mark Twain was. We are also,
despite all our familiar brashness, a deferential people,
and that is why it has taken us so long to discover how
amusing some of our most solemn thinking often can be.

Patience

"But the greatest of these is patience," said my friend over the telephone. He had been speaking of a difficult situation in his own life and I had been sympathizing. And I fell shortly afterward into reflection on that sober and pedestrian virtue. Patience, like charity, is long-suffering and kind. It is, moreover, the most practical of the virtues. For, with its aid and sustaining, all calamities can be endured, all fulfillments bearably and even hopefully awaited. Then, if the fulfillments do not come, patience itself has become a habit, and it renders the lack of fulfillment less hard to take, and the pain of privation more supportable.

My friend, himself a notable exemplar of this homely excellence, has with patience before now borne my borrowing of many of his ideas. He will not, I know (for nothing can de-philosophize him), be annoyed with me for filching this notion from him—as, I am sure, I have unknowingly filched many before. For it is only by a rare coincidence of honesty and alertness in one's psyche that one is aware clearly that an idea is not one's own.

Philosophy of the Swinging Pendulum

Things must seem normal again in many minds and in many households that have been living in an alien world since the 'thirties. The Republicans dominate Capitol Hill; the cry of "free enterprise" rises from the hills and the meadows—not to add, from the steel mills and chain stores of the land. The swing of the pendulum is relatively noiseless, but there are those who allege now that they can hear it plainly.

The philosophy of the swinging pendulum has now become rife. "The dialectic of history," Hegel once called it; and once it was called action and reaction. It is a comfortable notion, and one that may even lead to a pleasantly smug relaxation. Even those of us who cherish a few doubts about *laissez faire* can sit back now smugly, too, and await the *next* swing of the pendulum. Someday, say in another twelve years, there will be a new dispensation again. Who knows—even a new New Deal.

The pendulum swing is comfortable in the arts, too. Is there a movement toward abstraction in painting, and melody-less harmonies and harmony-less discords in music? Well, we who have lived long enough say to ourselves, "Just another ten or fifteen years now." Already one begins to notice in painting the reintrusion of themes and subject matter, and some of the most fanatically cerebral composers are lapsing into the comforting vulgarity of tunes again. Is poetry too crabbed and unintelligible? Softly, softly—wait but a little. The tintinnabulation of silver bells is beginning to stir again, and poets who have been beating themselves on the head in the hope of having something brainy and geometric occur to them are beginning to speak with feeling again; one ought not to be surprised that any day now one of them will have something to say that comes straight from the heart.

I should like to believe in the philosophy of the swinging pendulum, the dialectic of history, the inevitability of action and reaction. But on reflection, I do not think I do. I believe if the Bourbons were restored, even they would have learned a little and perhaps, blessedly, forgotten a little. Even the Ancien Regime, if re-established, would, I am sure, be a little less Ancien and a little more Moderne. I notice the Republicans are keeping a few controls; and even in music those who return to the eighteenth century return with some twentieth-century tone-colors and orchestral techniques. There is an old ritual dance in Luxembourg which is two steps forward and one backward. Time, falteringly, marches on.

(1947)

Portrait of a Lady

"I am," said the great lady, "terribly excited about existentialism. Of course," she added, "I don't quite know what it is." And she sighed. "I have done the best I can. I have read two articles in two different little reviews. I have forced my nephew, who is a graduate student in philosophy, to explain it to me, though the poor boy is frightfully addicted to long words. I have seen Sartre's play *No Exit,* which really has a very unpleasant set of characters in it. They are, as I understand it, in Hell, and I suppose one should not look for the best society there.

"I confess I am somewhat confused. It all goes back, back, apparently, to Kierkegaard, but there is some Nietzsche in it, too, and Pascal. I wish *Time* would sum it all up. They have such a gift for making things simple.

"The awful thing is, one wastes so much time on these things. Just as one is getting it straight in one's mind, the whole thing's gone out. I bought eight books on technocracy the season everybody was talking about that, and they still clutter up the limited book space in a New York apartment. And no one seems to talk about Gestalt psychology any more. Sometimes I think the intellectual life just isn't worth the trouble. By the way, what *is* existentialism?"

I told the great lady simply to wait serenely for six months, and the bother of asking the question, or even listening to the answer, would be spared her.

64

Brave New Busses

New York cannot be the only city which has a proud sense of being in the vanguard of civilization on no more profound grounds than that busses have been substituted for street cars. Celebration of progress, the new, accents the access of new virtues and amenities in our lives. It does not stress what we have lost. The old-fashioned street car moved in a stultified way along a perfectly straight line, which was satisfactory only to stodgy reactionaries who could, undisturbed, read stultifying editorials in unprogressive newspapers. The streetcars, too, exhibited only what Thorstein Veblen called "conspicuous waste." There was, relatively, a great deal of room in them. Some ancient citizens even remember the day when there was the vulgarly aristocratic service of having a separate man to collect one's fare after one was comfortably seated, not standing in a drafty doorway.

The busses doubtless are fine for keeping one pleasantly on the alert and on the qui vive. One keeps young, one *must* keep young to stand the wear and tear of being hurtled about in the zigzag foray of busses among the trucks and taxis. The busses, it is sometimes pointed out, too, are quieter and therefore infinitely more efficient as silent instruments of destruction. They can sneak up on pedestrians without the diffident waste motion of a warning.

One of the songs which (as the gossip columnists say)

my spies inform me is at this writing far up on the Hit
Parade is one that has the touching lines:

> He made the whole world brighter
> Wherever he would go,
> The old lamplighter
> Of long, long ago.

This year the lamplighter; last year there was a song
celebrating the trolley car. I myself recall my first definite
feeling against progress. It was when the soft glow of the
old Welsbach gas mantle was replaced by the hideous,
concentration-camp glare of the electric bulb. I think
there ought to be court orders "to show cause" when any
progressive movement is attempted or proposed. For
instance, there are people who are actually suggesting
that we substitute something for the nice, cozy, comfortable chaos of present civilization. World government!
United Nations! Well, all I can say is, that isn't the sweet,
familiar world of streetcars, gas lamps, wars, and depres-
sions in which I grew up. The gas lamp and the streetcar
are disappearing, but at least there is still violence, even
in times of peace; want in times of plenty; prejudice in
educated circles. I imagine progress won't be quite universal in our lifetime.

(1947)

Whose Contemporaries?

"I know," I said to the young man, "this is not the general opinion of your contemporaries."

"But aren't we all contemporaries?" he replied with uncalculated gallantry. And I began to reflect on who one's contemporaries really are. I know the best and the noblest theory on the subject, for I have been reading Emerson (Emerson on Plato). I know well enough that I am the contemporary of all men or of all kindred spirits in any age. I realize that Aeschylus and Dante speak to me across the centuries and, insofar as I am able to become one with their intention, they and I inhabit the same timeless moment.

Also, of late I have been reading some historical works, as for instance *The Age of Jackson* by Arthur Schlesinger, Jr. With help I have seen the parallels with the New Deal which (*eheu, fugaces!*) is now also in the past. Cicero's "On the Commonwealth," too, recently reread, reminds me that, in form and essence, historical periods are often twin brothers, if not identical twins.

But a university teacher, perhaps, is more prompted than other people to wonder who are his contemporaries in living fact, who are his immediate temporal brothers. If one loves the young, one flatters oneself that one's students are one's contemporaries. "In a university," Alfred North Whitehead once remarked, "a man's subject keeps his mind alive; his students keep his imagination alive." At their best, they remind one that this is always a young

67

world, and that there are ideas, even old ones, that are perpetually fresh. Once in a great while they remind older people that there are new ideas, even this late.

I have noticed in talking with my juniors that when the conversation runs to the nature of poetry or criticism, or Platonic ideas, it hardly enters into anyone's awareness that one interlocutor is fifty, the other twenty. But about more recent matters, including more recent books, the difference is serious. The young look back on Sherwood Anderson and Ernest Hemingway, when they do not look down on them. The middle-aged grew up with them, saw them flower into genius and fame.

When the talk between older and young men turns to talk of the future, the realized difference is even more serious. I find myself beginning to muse on what the world will be a generation from now, and two sobering reflections come into my mind. This younger contemporary before me will be a temporal brother, too, of that world a generation from now, and I, who am, in some measure at least, his contemporary, will not be contemporary with him and that world to come. But it is pleasant to think that on a few matters, and those the most winning and serious, the young and old can be contemporaries together—for yet a little while.

And Yet Again—Town Versus Country

Though the issue of town versus country was discussed by Plato in Athens and Horace in Rome, the theme was of sufficiently timely importance to merit a national discussion by radio on the "Town Meeting of the Air." The debate was, I take it, evoked by Mr. Granville Hicks's suggestive little book called *Small Town*. Various hands, all literate, took part; and, with a few variations, the arguments were such as might have been thought of, and indeed had been thought of, long ago in Greece and Rome. A piece of verse by Franklin P. Adams haunts my memory these many years:

> In summer I long for the winter
> With concerts in Carnegie Hall,
> In winter I long for the summer
> When there aren't any concerts at all.

The celebration of country life most often comes from the sophisticated, literary, and urban-minded. The joys of city life are as often noted by people nicely settled in the country! I have no desire to enter into the old argument, except to note the ancient suggestion that it would be agreeable to have the best features of each, which some of my friends manage to do by means of week ends. It may almost be said that civilization is coming to be the civilization of the week end—a state of ambiguity when one is at home neither in the country nor the city. But perhaps the flavor of the old argument for the city can be expressed by two images. There is a wonderful quietude about a city week end in summer—empty streets, a thin stream of traffic, when there is at once a rural peace and urban amenity. I am, on the other hand, reminded of the very urban friend of mine to whom I once said I was going to the country. He said amiably, "Well, have a good time, and kick a tree for me!"

The division of opinion will go on until the peril of the atomic bomb forces us all into the country. Or perhaps fear of what the atomic bomb may do to end city life will finally lead to doing something serious about controlling the atomic bomb.

Climate of Fact

The phrase "climate of opinion" has been rendered almost a standard part of the language, largely, I think, because of the currency given to it by Alfred North Whitehead. But there is a climate of fact, too, a weather of events by which even the most hardy or the most weatherbeaten are affected. Only three years ago, and it was not yet D-Day on the coasts of Normandy; and no one knew and everyone lived in suspense as to when that day would be. Only two years ago, and it began to look like the beginning of the end of the war in Japan. And just a little later, the atomic bomb fell on Hiroshima.

It is not only the climate of opinion that has changed, though the tone of things that it is common now, and was not common then, to say about Russia, for instance, has altered. But the facts about Russia and about many things, besides, have altered, too. Events shape not so much the direction as the range and area of our opinions. A world with atomic bombs in it, with postwar near-famine in most continents, with quarrels over Germany and over China and over Greece, with strikes at home and power politics in action abroad—this is, willy-nilly, the climate of fact in which we live. In more restricted fields a new atmosphere of fact is present, too; the colleges now have veterans in mufti where they once had soldiers in uniform. Where three years ago there were no students to be found, there are now not enough teachers. Three years ago there were shortages of everything from shirts to cigarettes; and now we begin to hear of collapsing markets and recession.

I have in my professional capacity talked a good deal about the necessity of detachment from the flux of events, and the possibility of attaining such detachment through philosophy. But what mind is unaffected by the vantage or disadvantage ground of the immediate present? The most age-spanning geological theory is uttered always in some here and now. Etruscan monuments are long since gone and remain a great mystery still. But a monograph on this remote subject published in 1947 would perhaps subtly reveal in some turn of phrase the date of the author's writing and the climate of present fact in which he looked at those remote inscrutable memorials.

(Summer, 1947)

◇◇◇

Weather in the Soul

There is weather in the spirit, too—often not directly traceable to the climate of fact. Who has not known a period of, say, a day, a week, a month, when everything seemed to go wrong, and nothing seemed to come out right? Life seems sometimes in a hundred exasperating little ways to be a conspiracy organized against one's own innocent and put-upon self. Work piles up in one dreadful and urgent mountain; a cold comes that cannot be thrown off; friends seem to clutter up one's week with a miscellany of obligations. A class meets, perhaps, or a succession of classes, in which the students seem singularly apathetic, and oneself preternaturally stupid. Then suddenly the weather clears, and all at once "mood and moment please" and one can "glimpse the fair Pierides."

Strength of Fools

I have a friend with whom I have had gentlemen's disagreements these many years about social and political and philosophical matters. He simply persists in having the wrong opinions, and, what is worse, repeatedly proffering them to me. It is, I have found, of little use to point out to him the errors of his intellectual ways. I remain astonished at his opaqueness to the clear paths to the improvement of his understanding which I have mapped out for him. He is simply and smugly and literally incorrigible. One would think that by this time he would see the good sense of my opinions instead of remaining obdurately fixed in his own ways, as an Irish friend of mine puts it, "like a pig at a dance." As for me, I have never understood why he does not admire my laudable consistency. I am irritated that he does not marvel at the way in which I so many years ago lighted upon the unmistakable truth. He is very stubborn, really, and perversely blind. He is visiting me tonight. I must try just once again.

On Hearing a Pin Drop

Many must have had the experience, at once quiet and tense, of sitting before a microphone in a radio studio in the thirty seconds before a program is about to go on the air. It makes no difference whether one is participating in the program or not. There is an awed hush about the studio, as if it were the eve of a transcendental revelation, as if at the end of half a minute some final insight or ultimate judgment were to be delivered. There are other reasons for the tension, of course. Everyone present, including the hard-boiled radio engineers and the casually calloused announcers, have the terrible fear (immortalized in many a classic radio anecdote) that some untoward word, some *negligé* private observation, intended for the intimacy of the studio or the control room only, may be heard by thousands or millions over a national network.

It is bad enough if one is only a visitor, but it is worse by far, as I have found out, if one is actually participating on a broadcast. In some ways, speaking over the radio is the least taxing of forms of public address. It is hardly necessary to raise one's voice; the radio engineers take care of that. If there is no studio audience, it is as simple as soliloquizing in a study. But in the moment just before going on the air, there comes a terrible, brief *crise de nerfs*. In a moment one is going to speak into the unknown, and perhaps split an infinitive in the ears of who knows how many, who knows where. If it is a program without a script, the thought comes: "Suppose, with all those listening ears, I shall have *nothing* at all to say." In the excitement, it hardly enters the mind that there may not *be* any listening ears.

The minute before going off the air is equally tense, too. There is a tradition in radio that one must hit it "on the nose," and end promptly with the sharply defined half-hour of the radio clock. And then the uneasy tiny interval. Is one off the air yet or not? Dare one speak in normal relaxed tones? Is it certain that there are but a handful of flesh-and-blood listeners, not the assumed ghostly millions? "You could hear a pin drop" used to be the last word about silence. A new metaphor is now in order: "It was silent in the room, as if everyone in it were about to go on the air." I presume one is not allowed to drop a pin in a radio studio. Probably it sounds like the clang of a prison gate.

Hardy Perennial

Commencements will flourish again this year, and the Commencement orators will flourish, too. The tone, I suspect, will be more Cassandra than Pollyanna, or, more likely, Matthew Arnold, this year. Sweetness and light will yield place to warnings and alarums. I wonder if it will really make much difference to the young in any case. The Commencement address is part of the time-honored ritual (like the word "time-honored"). Eloquence on such occasions has a certain suasion, and wit—possibly because it is not anticipated—is doubly welcome. Once in a century an address may be a classic, like Emerson's "The American Scholar" or, to a lesser degree, Woodrow Wilson's neglected classic "The Spirit of Learning." But I cannot believe that the young, generally, are much affected by the substance of what is said on such occasions. The newest Phi Beta Kappa members are still too set up by their recent distinction, the current bachelors of arts by their immediate problems of love or their summer jobs. They are anesthetized by the voice of Polonius from the older generation, whether it be disguised as Cassandra or Pollyanna.

In my own college generation, the tone of Commencement addresses was generally optimistic; today it is likely to be grim and foreboding. The young were not too much impressed then, nor will they be too much depressed now. But people miss a great many sermons in church these days. It is good to have a secular sermon

77

now and then, particularly in the long slanting light of a late afternoon in June, outdoors on an ivy-clad campus, in the shadow of a chapel. It makes no difference what the tone of the address; the tones themselves, albeit of a trustee, at such a time, in such a place, in such a mood, are musical.

Quieter, Please

The other day I picked up an earnest noncommercial periodical which boasted an article whose title contained the phrase "dynamic democracy." There are certain words that have come to be used in our time as terms of implied moral praise. "Dynamic" is one of these, "vitality" another, and "life" itself is intended to connote a value and a good. I confess these words always make me a little uneasy. They are virtually accusations of lethargy and deliberate torpor. At the end of a long day or at the beginning of a rainy one, to pick up an essay that feverishly exhorts one to "dynamic democracy" or to "vital philosophy" or to "living thought" or to "creative individuality" is a shock and a kind of indictment. As this is written, it is a dark, dull, foggy morning without the slightest trace of anything "dynamically creative" or "vital" about it—or in my own psyche. I know if I were worth preserving in the world, I should snap into "creativeness" and burst with "dynamicness." I often envy the writers of such homilies, though I cannot help wishing some of the qualities they recommend would overflow into their own prose. The tones in which they counsel such exuberant virtues are like the gray in the sky this dull morning.

By the time these lines get into print, I hope everybody, including the reader, is feeling "dynamic"; that is the "vital" thought with which I should like to close this meditation.

The Déjà Vu

People in academic life are, I think, peculiarly likely to be afflicted with the sense of perpetual recurrence, and the consciousness, not altogether happy, of having seen all this before. The beginning of one college year is much like the beginning of all other academic years: the students milling about for registration, the half-skeptical, half-interested curiosity of a hundred upturned faces at a first lecture in a new course, the stream of advisees. Even an "original" student is original somehow in ways reminiscent of some maverick of ten years ago. Then there is the meeting of colleagues, with the familiar exchange of greetings and the mutual confessions of the summer having passed without one's having accomplished more than half of what one had planned. Do farmers yawn a little at the return of the seasons or the birds? Perhaps not, and academic people do not yawn either at the beginning of the year. They are much too busy. But even in the midst of a crowded day the same sense of the thrice familiar must assail them.

There is a comfort in it, too, a dangerous solace. The world may be headed for destruction, but, for the time being at least, classes meet Monday and Wednesday at eleven, the dean's office sends out the usual notices, the curriculum is about to be revised again. How snug (and how easily smug) a little world it is to slip back into.

Hermitage de Luxe

A hotel room in a standard hotel in a strange city where one knows no one, a bedroom in a transcontinental train —these are my notions of retreat, escape, privacy, solitude. They are the true hermitage for the modern man. I know of some people who go to a hotel in their own city once in a while just to get away from it all, but there is a delusion about that. One walks out into the familiar world with doubtless a relative or a chore just around the corner. No, a hotel in a strange city, or a room, not a berth, on a modern train—that is the authentic luxury of isolation. All the better that the cell in the train, the room in the hotel, is standardized. One is on the essence of all trains, one is in any hotel in any city in the land or almost on the globe.

For the time being, one is away from the very things one loves—but which have become so intimately one's self that they are wearisomely identified with, and exhaustingly as well as exhaustively define, one's self. Here in Room 1402 of the Hotel —— (the name does not matter in a city whose whereabouts do not count) where these lines are written, I might be anywhere or everywhere. I hate to leave. I become attached to this featureless anonymity. On a train it is even better, for the room is reduced to bleak and functional simplicity; all save the upholstery is cool, clean Pullman steel. And one has the sensation, more than in an airplane, of moving very fast to vague important destinations.

I should not, I confess, like this regimented isolation very long. This is too anonymous a nirvana, and too impersonal a nothingness. There is quite a difference, despite Plotinus, between being one with the One and being alone with the Alone. But for the time being it is bliss to be alive, to be alone is Heaven.

Dial Tone

"Wait until you hear the dial tone," the telephone company admonishes, "or you will not be able to make your connection." Sometimes the dial tone is heard at once, and there is a pleasure in the recognition, a sense that all is well. I have long cherished the belief that in reading one has a similar experience. In the first page, sometimes in the first paragraph, of a writer whom one has never read before, one is aware, in the tone and cadence of the sentences themselves, that one has the dial tone, or, perhaps, that the connection has been made. There will doubtless be a good deal about the book that will be a disappointment: perhaps the tone will be lost or the connection broken. But what a thrill it is to come upon it, if for the moment only.

I am prepared to accept all manner of explanation of the phenomenon. Obviously it is often dependent on the state of well-being of the reader. Given a high enough euphoria in the reader, and the Congressional Record or a report of the Department of Agriculture could give such a note. But I have learned seldom to distrust a first impression. Something about the movement, the melody, the rhythm of the sentences tells me within half a minute that I am in the presence of authentic writing, not manufactured or faked, but the unmistakable lifeblood of literature.

Uncommon Man

Paul occasionally drops in upon me, full of ideas about history, about philosophy, about human nature. He is particularly refreshing because in his business, which is entertainment, he is not given to the current jargon of the schools, and his own schooling is limited. But he is filled with large and generous notions about man and the universe, and he has a wide ruminative historical imagination—say, like Toynbee's. "Human beings have been," he announced to me the other day, "trying for a long time to avoid taking the rap which was given them originally on account of Adam and Eve. Ever since, they have been trying to palm off the punishment, to pass the buck to someone else. First it was slaves, the conquered, then the poverty-stricken, and women and kids. Always there has been some class trying to make some other class pay the freight. The rich pass off the burdens to the poor, men to women, the conquerors to the conquered, adults to children, the big shots to the little fellows. But with human progress, one group after another has refused to take it. One way of understanding democracy is this: it is a way of life which realizes that we must all take the rap together, that we are in the same boat. We *must* take the rap, that's what it is to be human; we must all take it, that's what democracy is."

"Sure, use the idea," Paul said. "I don't even know enough to know if it's mine."

84

Cerebral Hygiene

Auguste Comte, as almost everybody knows, believed in having a period of cerebral hygiene, when the mind was given a vacation from printed matter. But merely stopping reading is not necessarily a true washing out of the spirit. Out, out damned print! All one has to do is to stop reading for a while, to see how much one's mind and imagination have been stamped by what one has read of late or long ago.

More striking than being cut off from books is being cut off, as I am for a time this summer, from letters. There is nothing like being alone in a strange place away from one's friends even by mail (and, illusorily, cut off from one's obligations, too) to teach one how social a fabrication is one's life. Everything is happily remote for the time being. No editor can hurry a manuscript, no dean a report, no friend a reply. There is the half-sweet, half-bitter illusion of being alone, isolate in a friendless region, and at ease in a world where there are no responsibilities. At this remove in the evergreen Northwest, I have a hard time persuading myself there is a home I have to go to, a New York in which it exists.

Dead-Pan

A correspondent once wrote me anent the comments which appear some pages back concerning a stubborn friend who for years has stupidly refused to realize how wise and true my opinions are, and has persisted in his own errors with what I called the strength of fools. My correspondent says, apparently seriously, that the trouble with such satiric comment is that most people take it too literally, and that someday I shall find that something I have spoken with my tongue in my cheek is taken at its face meaning.

There is evidence to support the lady's point. The New York *Sun* under Charles Dana was famous for its ironic editorials. But it could never publish one without having dozens of letters pour in from readers who recognized no ironic intent. I suspect that if one were to organize a society for the extinction of the human race on the ground that if there were no human race there could be no human miseries, a certain number of persons would be persuaded to join the organization, while a certain number of others would protest the callousness or the logical absurdity of the scheme.

David Low, the cartoonist, in his introduction to a collection of his witheringly genial picture commentaries on our times, remarked that the satirist has lost his vocation. For there is nothing, he says, so silly or fantastic or incredible or savage or stupid that some dictator or fraud of our time has not actually put it into practice. No wonder the satirist is well advised to be careful. It is hard to know these days what is said as a joke and what is said dead-pan. For instance, one hears in high quarters that universal military training is the only insurance of peace. In the light of the history of the last hundred years in Europe, it is hard when one hears such an opinion to know whether it is said in earnest or not. One man's faith is another man's farce.

The Middle Half

I have been hearing liberals complain that their lot in the present world is an extremely difficult one. They are reviled and misunderstood by the extremists of both the Left and Right. If they plead for socialized medicine, they are Communists, and if they point out the abuses among labor union leaders, they are Fascists. No one seems to understand what high and reasonable middle-of-the-road men they are. But I wonder whether there is anything new about the distrust of the liberal position in politics, or in morals. In a time when lines are being severely drawn, it is easy to ask, "Are you for us or against us?" A middle course looks like evasion of ultimate issues.

But has it not been so always? Even in the eighteenth century, I suspect the "reasonable" man must have got on a lot of people's nerves—even those of cultivated and reasonable people. There is nothing much one can do about it either, in the way of propaganda. One cannot glamorize the life of reason, for that would convict us of "enthusiasm." It is not cricket to be "excited" about decency and order and integrity. It is sentimental to place too much hope on or in good sense. Tolerance has been one of the virtues of the liberal creed. One can only trust the world will permit tolerance itself to continue. If not, liberalism will certainly die, and with it possibly the most distinctively human quality of Western man.

Homesick for Heaven

The nostalgia industry is growing by leaps and bounds. In plays, in novels, in autobiographies and softly retrospective histories, our eyes are asked to wander back over fairer vistas only a generation old, but now psychologically a part of prehistory.

It is coming to appear now that just around the turn of the century the most comfortable forms of bliss were epidemic. Magic carpets in the form of bicycles enabled one to ride, with decent slowness, moderate distances through unspoiled countryside. There were huge dinners, punctuated halfway through by Roman punch, to give a cooling interval so that one could apply oneself freshly to the second part of the grandiose meal. Gentlemen—and little boys—wore proper stiff collars. Streetcars clattered deliciously along cobblestoned streets. Life was uncorrupted by ice cubes, automobiles, subways. There were no income taxes (or social security); there were no noisy airplanes overhead—also, it must be admitted, no "miracle" drugs.

Obviously even the most nostalgic, when pressed, will make two admissions: if they are old enough actually to remember, they recall many of the discomforts and inconveniences of a now softly fabled past; they know also, as many a middle-class child knew when occasionally he passed through slums, that the notion of universal security and serenity was a myth for all but the comfortable classes—and a myth, too, for some members of those classes. Around 1900, even the small boy could detect the tensions and insecurities in a so-called "happy family." We did not in those days have the language of Freud to help us understand, but there were other languages of understanding simpler and not altogether simple-minded.

There is more than one variety of historical homesickness—the heart, disenchanted with the present, has turned back to the Middle Ages, to Greece, to the Garden of Eden. But the current mode is a yearning for the *immediate* past. The last generation is gilded in the memories of those who spent their childhood in it. It is aureoled also for younger people, who trustingly believe the sentimental tales of their elders, and are quite ready to agree that fifty years ago must certainly have been better than the present, and at least could not have been worse. It is perfectly clear that around 1900 nobody except eccentric fanatics thought the world might be coming to an end any minute. The insane dreams of a generation ago have become standard sanity now.

At all times of desperation and crisis, people have had to look to "a world elsewhere." It might as well be the world of yesterday. A dreamed-of Heaven may be placed anywhere, any time. Yesterday is as good a spot for Heaven as tomorrow, and Utopia, perhaps to the surprise of those who remember Lot's wife, is sometimes most vividly seen by a backward glance.

Now What on Earth For?

I saw a personal advertisement the other day—I really did—which called for "an astrologer, young, who speaks French and is willing to travel."

At odd moments since I have tried to imagine for what on earth such a singularly equipped individual was required. I have speculated on the matter briefly at the end of a long day, when it was impossible to think more responsibly on more urgent matters.

It occurs to me that some wealthy retired financier whose whole fortune had been made under the guidance of astrologers at moments of crisis (the idea is not fantastic; in the 'twenties many eminent Wall Street financiers were reputed to consult astrologers) now wished to spend a year or two in traveling around the globe. Since income taxes in the higher income brackets are what they are, even a retired tycoon cannot afford to take along one of the expensive, well-established astrologers. Doubtless he hoped to find some young man in the profession whose rates were still reasonable and who would enjoy a year or two of travel. And since the astrologer will surely be vigorous as well as young, he may also serve as a courier, and in primitive parts of the world even be able to protect his patron in moments of physical danger.

The matter of the French requirement continued to puzzle me for a while. Why *must* the astrologer speak French, which is no longer, in the old eighteenth-century sense, the universal language? I have finally arrived at an explanation of that prerequisite too; my financier had at the end of his junior year in Yale spent a summer in France, and had come to be able to spell out the menus and make himself understood by taxi drivers. He had reached the conclusion that French was a very elegant language, and that someday he would give himself an opportunity to practice it. He had, indeed, gone to the Berlitz School for a year in his youth. It occurred to me that he might have simplified matters by advertising for a French astrologer, but he was a modest man and he, perhaps felt that *his* French was not good enough really for a Frenchman. Now, a young astrologer who could speak French was exactly what was required. Hence, I am sure, the advertisement.

Having decided which, I found myself re-energized for serious work.

On Advantages Not Taken

Once last summer, while I was living for a few weeks in a small prairie town in Montana, I ruminated a little bit on all the things in New York I should be missing were I fated to live away from it always: the concerts, the interesting visitors always turning up, the theaters, the exhilaration of gossip about all the kinds of work and play that go on in a metropolis, the occasional parties, or dinners, the sharpening give-and-take of an international center. An English novelist, a South African philosopher, a Portuguese soprano—one never knows whom one is going to meet next in New York.

As for music and the theater, quite apart from the routine programs of the symphony orchestras and the Broadway playhouses, there are the series of "little concerts," chamber music, and Spanish guitarists, and neglected Bach cantatas put on by small churches, and the latest existentialist drama provided by an experimental theater. And the French and British movies, and the innumerable art exhibitions on Fifty-seventh Street. I thanked God I was not geographically placed like other men.

Now, in the midst of the ordinary obligations of the working year in New York, I still think of all these wonderful opportunities and the number of them—the majority of them, in fact—which I shall be missing. It is something, of course, to be virtually right around the corner from all the stimulation of art and music and society in the greatest city in the world. It is a wry pleasure to be so *closely* reminded of all that one is missing. Or *is* it a pleasure at all? There is said to be a strain about life in New York. I think I'm beginning to see now what it is. In Montana I should not be torn in one evening between the Ballet Theatre and three Beethoven quartets—or work.

Is There Any News?

"Is there any news?" How many times I have been asked that by old friends. My answer depends very little on the general state of the world. What a friend wants to know when he asks such a question is what has happened in our little mutual world. Deaths, marriages, books published or completed—or projected, jobs acquired or old ones relinquished. The answer I actually make doesn't even have much to do with the news current in the parochial cosmos in which the inquirer and I both live. It depends largely on my own state of well-being. There are days when even the tiniest events seem shining with interest, and the smallest trivia fit to repeat as if they were a revelation. But there are wintry days, too, when, crack my brains as I will, I can find nothing that anyone will, by a remote stretch of good will, want to hear, or anything I can manage to tell without yawning.

"No, no news," I say, "nothing at all; everything about as usual," on the very day that a radio announcer tells of a rocket plane, of the increasing threat of war, of hurricane in the Caribbean and famine in India. But then, those things are in essence, I suppose, not news. There have always been wars and rumors of wars. Some day though, when the phone rings, it would be nice to be able to say breathlessly, "But of *course!* Haven't you heard? The millennium, coming tomorrow. But I'll tell you about it when I see you. How about lunch, at the club, twelve-fifteen?"

Far Away and Long Ago

The letter in an unfamiliar handwriting said that I probably did not recall the writer, but that twenty years ago in Switzerland at Pontresina she, then a young girl, and I had spent the afternoon discussing Plotinus and neo-Platonic philosophy, about which she had known nothing and which she did not very much understand, and in which, as she said, she had not pretended any particular interest. I tried desperately hard to remember the girl, the occasion, and the circumstances under which I would have spent a whole afternoon talking about Plotinus with someone who was not in the least interested. Try as I would, I could not recollect. There was a period, I remember, when I had just discovered that intellectual mystic, and was trying to convert some of my positivistic and materialistic friends to a perception of his wisdom. But what I must have thought I was doing in the beautiful upland meadows of the Engadine, explaining Plotinus to a bored young lady, I cannot imagine. She claimed in her letter not to have been bored, and I suppose that is what she claimed at the time. I am sure that is why I spent the afternoon explaining the author of the idea that the height of felicity was "To be Alone with the Alone." It was a very rude idea to celebrate the delights of absolute solitude to a lovely girl in a lovely place.

Variation from a Theme

The seventeen-year-old boy had come to me partly on his own instigation and partly on that of his father, a house-painter. I had not looked forward too much to the interview for, as I understood it, it was something about entering college and something, also, about a poor high school record. I did not anticipate with pleasure the prospect of having to tell the young man it was hard enough to get into a good college—or any college—with a poor high school record at any time, but especially so these days.

The youth came in, looking shy and troubled and rather winning in a not too brilliant way.

"Ah, he knows," I said to myself, "that he is asking help in a rather difficult matter."

He was asking aid, but not about what I expected. "Could you help me," he said earnestly, soon after we began talking, "to persuade my parents that I *oughtn't* to go to college?"

The habits of a lifetime made me, almost automatically, start to remind him of the values of a liberal education, how important the great books were, what a resource it was in time of trouble and unhappiness to have the arts and science and philosophy as a refuge. I glanced at him and checked myself. It was a safe bet he had already had some experience in the great books, had already been bored to death by *Hamlet* and *Macbeth* and Homer, had had a chance over WQXR to feed

97

his soul on Beethoven and Mozart—and had already re-jected these golden opportunities. Who was I to urge him to have some more of these (to him) unpalatable goods stuffed down his throat? It turned out in the course of further conversation that what the boy wanted des-perately to be was a dental technician, and that the thought of college was nothing less than revolting to him. His parents, I gathered, felt very strongly that he should have the blessings of higher education, even though he found them a curse.

The situation put a college teacher in an embarrassing spot. "In the confidence of this room," I felt like saying, "don't go to college. Stick by your guns. Be a pure and unsullied dental technician. Don't let them force a higher life upon you. But don't tell anybody I said so." Instead, I was academically fair-minded. In the best tradition of the noncommittal, I pointed out the advantages of both sides, knowing the admissions offices of the colleges would probably settle the boy's problem for him.

One never knows what ripples one's falling pebble will stir up. A few days later I met the boy's father. "My boy wants to come to see you again," he said. "He says you made college sound very nice."

Ground for Suspicion

Apropos of I cannot remember what, my colleague re-marked at lunch, "I am always suspicious of people who are in a hurry." I carefully refrained from looking at my watch, as I had been about to do, and ostentatiously lingered over the coffee. But later my friend's observation returned to haunt me. I began to reflect on the grounds for his suspicion. He had not, I am certain, sin-ister disquietudes in mind. He did not mean that he thought any of his hurried and harried friends were on their hasty way to the performance of illegal errands. They were probably innocently racing to cubicles in li-braries, or to their typewriters, or to meetings organized with the most generous intent for the best of causes. He had, I am certain, subtler grounds for suspicion, and I find myself beginning to share them.

Obviously one ought to suspect a man who is perpetu-ally in a hurry. He patently has had no time to stop and reflect what it is he is in a hurry about. He is likely also to be an extraordinarily unperceptive and unsympathetic character. He has no time to enjoy the things or persons from whom he is continually hurrying away. Obviously a man who can scarcely stop to say "hello" is treating you as a way station rather than as a terminal point. Lei-sure, as Aristotle pointed out, is a good because it makes contemplation possible. The hurried man allows him-self no leisure. By Heavens! I am myself now beginning to be completely suspicious of people in a hurry. They have no time for enjoyment, for contemplation, or even for sleep or good manners. If I did not have other pressing and immediate obligations, I should like to develop this theme, possibly into a book. I begin to be suspicious of myself.

The Age of Facsimile

A while ago I had the pleasure of being invited to dinner by a young couple, both veterans of the Navy. They are now both students. Under the difficult conditions of the tiniest of kitchenettes and the slowest of electric stoves, the young wife had provided an excellent dinner initiated by a soup with a rare and delightful flavor. "How fortunate an age we are living in," I said to myself, "when a busy young woman can provide, out of a can, so exotically interesting a soup, one that would have been attainable earlier only at an expensive French restaurant or after hours of labor."

"This is wonderful," I said after a mouthful.

The young housekeeper blushed with pleasure. "It is made from an old recipe that has been in our family for two generations," she said. "It's quite a lot of trouble to prepare and it takes a long time, but when it turns out it is worth it."

It was on the tip of my tongue to say that it was just as good as the biggest and best corporation could produce, and that it was wonderful that she, an inexperienced young woman, should be able to compete so successfully with the research chefs of large corporations.

How often one meets analogous circumstances. The corrupted taste of the present age cherishes similar experience. At a Saturday matinee of the Boston Symphony in New York I once heard a dowager lady say to a friend that this live performance of Haydn's symphony sounded almost as real and almost as good as the Boston records of the symphony she had played that morning. I heard a young man, prompted to read *Great Expectations* by the movie version of it, say, apparently seriously, that the book almost caught the spirit of the movie. There are, I am told, people who find football games and prize fights much less authentic on the field and in the ring than they do in the bona fide of television. This sort of thing has been growing, possibly most rapidly since the ubiquity of the telephone. At a crowded cocktail party a while ago, I ran into an old friend I had not seen in months. "It is impossible to talk here in all this crush," he said. "I'll telephone you tomorrow and we'll have a real good heart-to-heart chat over the phone."

Family Retainer

I was rather startled to hear the well-known lady novelist speak within ten minutes of my meeting her of "my analyst," as she might have spoken of her coiffeur or her laundryman or her doctor. There was in her voice, as she spoke of her analyst, the same mixture of attitudes as she might have used about others in her service. Her analyst was a combination of father confessor, service station, confidant, friend, repairman, personnel counselor, and private tutor. She spoke, in fact, of being in the process of taking a "refresher analysis."

I hasten to disclaim any easy and arrogant dismissal of analysis either as theory or therapy. I am simply noting the fact that, in the sociology of our time, psychological analysis as treatment often appears in the context of middle-class luxuries—one of the ways of keeping up with the Joneses. The thing becomes a real luxury when, as in the case of certain fabled tycoons, it is possible to speak of "my private analyst." Of course, the perfect luxury would be a private analyst transported everywhere in a private plane.

All this indicates, as any indignant, satisfied patient of analysis will tell me, my own patent need for analysis. But a very reputable analyst told me recently that professional intellectuals are the worst possible patients, and that beyond a certain age they are practically hopeless. That is perhaps what makes me scoff. No one, apparently, will be *my* analyst.

It Is Earlier Than You Think

I suddenly realize that I have been rebelling against the whole pressure psychology implied by the ominous phrase "it is later than you think." It is obvious that the expression is intended to waken us from our lethargies, to recall us to the urgency of the things that need to be done if we or the human race are to survive at all. The phrase, now practically standard cliché, is meant to remind us that chaos is further along than we realize, that anarchy is approaching a climax, that our enemies have the secret of the atomic bomb, or that our own bombs are on the point of explosion. The incantation is intended to recall to us the fact that racial intolerance has mounted more rapidly than we are content to acknowledge, or than in a year or two we will be able to counteract; that we shall any moment now be drowned by the tide of inflation—to sum it all up briefly, that any instant now we will be inundated by irretrievable despair. There is, of course, no doubt that it is very late indeed with respect to all these things. It is late, and we are not thinking at all. There are hurricane warnings, and we blandly ignore them; there are telltale signs of young earthquakes, and we blithely or stubbornly refuse to notice them. It is thus probably a very good thing to be admonished that the sands are running out, but I have begun to wonder just how good a thing it really is to hear repeatedly this portentous-with-foreboding tocsin. Instead of instigating action, it helps to paralyze it. If one believes it is so hysterically late, one is tempted to throw up one's hands. What is to be done in so little time?

Not so long ago people were talking about the "wave of the future." If it is really as late as people say, one might be tempted to let the wave roll over us and over everything. We have come into the habit, moreover, of talking glibly about the end of an era—a habit of speech which the emphasis on the lateness of the hour confirms. Some era in something is ending every day—which is, of course, to say that some era in something is day by day beginning.

Might not it be a useful therapeutic propaganda for a while to be reminded that in important ways it is earlier than we think? When we are told that Western civilization is bankrupt, it would be helpful and even true to observe that on a geological and biological scale Western civilization is extremely young. When we are informed that the human race is politically and socially at its wits' end, it would be encouraging perhaps to have it noted that human intelligence, especially in its scientific form, has been applied to social and political affairs for a paltry hundred years or so. When we are told that it is nearly midnight and that doom will come on the stroke of that fateful hour, it might help to have it retorted that it is only dawn, and early dawn—in which one cannot see very clearly. Really, it *is* rather earlier than we think —not early enough to go back to sleep, but to relax tension a little, with still time perhaps to get something done.

◇◇◇

There's a Reason

Among the random impressions of my childhood, there is an advertisement that used to appear on the platforms along the elevated railroad stations in New York. It was the slogan of a breakfast food that was spelled in large letters, and it was a slogan that did nothing to explain the virtues of the cereal advertised. It said simply and decisively and vaguely, "There's a reason." It seemed to my ten-year-old mind somehow very impressive. I was quite prepared to believe that there was a reason and a good one, and of course even in that day it was not hard to have sense enough to conclude that the slogan meant a reason for eating that particular breakfast food, or a reason for its special virtue.

I have often noted since then, in adult life, that in the course of discussion on matters social or economic or religious there will be the intimation, too, that there is a reason. The reason is often implied rather than stated. Carried far enough, the argument runs, of course, that there is a reason in and for the universe, though only the slightest acquaintance with traditional theology is needed to realize that the reason is often left quite unspecified—even the reason that there should be a reason. Only the other day I listened to a philosophical paper in which the author said with passionate conviction, "Perhaps ideas beyond our comprehension ought to be our principles of comprehension."

I am less prepared than I was as a child reading the

breakfast food advertisement to accept the allegation that there is a reason. I am sure that there is reason for my skepticism. Any anthropologist, psychiatrist, or sociologist, given my psycho-biography, my economic environment, and the "age of anxiety" I live in, could give it. But I do not think they should be distracted from larger issues.

How Is Everything?

In the middle of a busy day when a good many minor things had gone mildly wrong, I ran into someone I had known long and casually who hailed me with a revolting cheerfulness by asking gaily, "Well, how is everything?" The very tone of the inquiry intimated his expectation that "everything" was just fine and dandy, or that I would at the very least briefly declare that it was. A bore is one who, when you ask him how he feels, tells you in detail.

The omnipresent intrusion of the radio has perhaps taught us to listen to words and to discount their meaning. Even apart from radio, social life is marked by the use of conventional inquiries to which purely nominal replies are expected. My questioner certainly did not really want to know how *everything* was, either in the state of the world in general or in my own life. I was tempted, like the Ancient Mariner, to fix and hold him, and for once in a way start in at least to tell him how everything was so far as I knew, from atomic energy and the Russians to the momentary mood of my own psyche in the singularly lucid nightmare I had had in the way of a dream the night before.

As it was, I felt impelled at least to give a rational though brief answer, to explain that as to how everything was, the bleak truth was that some things were good and some things were bad, and that roughly speaking and in a necessarily hasty attempt to summarize the whole situation, everything was on the whole, if not fine and dandy, not quite unbearable. I had not given up in despair as to the future of civilization, nor on more personal grounds had I been tempted to throw myself from a high place, turn on the gas, plunge into the Hudson, to imprison myself in a closed car, or perish from carbon monoxide. "Oh, I guess everything's fine and dandy," I found myself saying.

My questioner knew that was not so, and I do not think cared very much; and I knew it was not so, and did not scruple about lying. Routine social conversation oscillates between the false and the meaningless. That alone is not so fine, but, for the sake of brevity, everything else is.

The Victim of Propaganda

Like everybody else, I have been increasingly impressed by the fact that so much of what we read about public affairs, or even affairs that are relatively less public, is propaganda. By this time it is almost impossible to read a headline about Russia, Israel, Czechoslovakia, Yugoslavia, not to add Guatemala, Ecuador, and Heligoland, without wondering who has wished to say what why. A century ago liberal thinkers regarded the press as a great instrument of democratic education; and newspaper publishers, addressing dinners of the NAM today, still repeat these pious optimisms. But we have been informed, perhaps over-informed, that practically everything is propaganda. The other night over the radio I heard what years ago I might have thought was an innocent weather report. The announcer said that a depression had settled over Iceland and was moving slowly south. A canard, probably put out by Moscow.

Most of us, I think, rather smugly feel that if there is propaganda in any alleged news item or even in some meditative nostalgic reminiscence by Sir Osbert Sitwell, we are so alert and alerted that we can recognize it. I myself have the comfortable conviction that by careful and sophisticated reading, and by a nice and expert discounting of obvious propaganda, I can get the substantial truth about Russia, Israel, Czechoslovakia, Yugoslavia, Guatemala, Ecuador, and Heligoland. It is a little as if all the talk about propaganda had proved a self-corrective for distortion, so that one is about where one was.

The propagandists have overdone it so much that the fairly intelligent reader feels that by taking a little trouble he can get at the facts pretty well, even now. He feels he has learned to translate double-talk into single-mindedness, and knows on the whole exactly what everybody means, no matter what he says. It is the same technique that people pride themselves on mastering when with a smattering of psychoanalysis they manage to pay no attention to the surface meaning of what people say, but substitute complete awareness of what they know, in the now-obvious recesses of their subconscious, people really mean. Fooled by propaganda? Indeed! What! *Me?*

Progress

I am aware of course that progress is no longer fashionable. I do not mean that people have given up wishing for improvement, but the belief that there is any genuine improvement in the world to look forward to has been gradually collapsing since the eighteenth century. Yet, in our private worlds, how we continue to believe about certain particular things that everything is getting better and better, and how we look with un-nostalgic disdain on our former estimation of goods and perfections!

These reflections on the theory of progress are brought to my mind by the fact that I am now the happy possessor of what I regard as the last word in musical reproduction. I am the owner of an instrument, whose name I shall provide on request, which is happily in and not out of this world. I am, of course, convinced that all previous musical reproduction is practically in the paleolithic stage. What is more, I recall how I have felt this each time I have had the privilege of listening to a somewhat better machine—since the days when I first heard the sort of instrument that is still pictured in the advertisements, that representing an astonished and faithful dog listening to his master's voice coming out of a horn.

There was a succession of improvements: the conical horn, and then the horn put in a box (but it sounded, so we told ourselves, ever so much better); then there was the age of improved "accoustical" reproduction; then the major revolution of electrical reproduction (so that within a year everybody who merely owned an acoustical phonograph was regarded as living in the Tobacco Road of music), and now this transcended perfection—which, as I explained to a friend the other day, makes the music sound really better than it is when heard in the concert hall, and glorifies it in a way that the actual performance could not possibly do. It is all nonsense, this modern fashion to disbelieve in progress. Things, at any rate, are getting better and better—even if their owners are not.

The Frontiers of Credulity

During weeks of a varying succession of sleet, snow, and rain, it seems almost impossible to believe that it will ever be green and warm again. It is no use having somebody trot out the familiar "If Winter comes, can Spring be far behind?" The fact is that one is quite certain it can be very far behind indeed; there are damp, penetrating, desperate undertaker-days when one is sure spring will never catch up at all.

Now to the rational mind, of course, this is absurd. There have been bad winters before, and it is perfectly patent after a moment's reflection that the probability that spring, and even summer, will come, is so great that even a chastened weather bureau would call it a certainty. The fact is that what is difficult is not intellectual assent but pictorial imagination. It is discouraging to think that there will be a certain low point of morale every winter when the conviction of an eventual summer will seem quite impossible, and strain as one will, one cannot see as imminent Falstaff's babble of green fields.

Unfortunately, this is true not only about the physical weather, but about the moral and political weather of the world. In this "winter of our discontent" through which we are living, in the sleet, the hail, the rain, and the intense cold of postwar confusion and disillusion, it is also impossible to believe that there will be a spring-tide in the affairs of men, or ever a full and radiant summer. It is no use, again, for the rational mind to remind itself that scientific method and democracy are both very young, and that in the long run, given a chance, they will come to united triumph.

The tired liberal is a familiar phenomenon. He was present after the last war, and his fears and wariness *then* seem to have been justified. It is not that the liberal mind is crushed, but that the liberal imagination is flattened out. It takes almost impossible effort these days even to imagine a world at peace. It is even more difficult to imagine a world in anything better than the uneasy equilibrium of tensions ready to snap.

It has become the fashion to smile a little at romantic hopes for the world, or Utopias of a perfect society. But it could be that it is precisely such dreams and visions that are needed to rekindle the fagged enthusiasms of man. It is hard to believe, but it is even harder to imagine, to see, as seers and poets see. A few poets and prophets helping us to *see* would fortify our belief that in the moral and political world too, however severe the winter, some spring, however late, will come.

On Watching the Self

A little while ago, during an attack of the grippe, I was given by my doctor a mild sleeping tablet which he had prescribed in answer to my complaint that a cough kept me restlessly awake. He was quite enthusiastic about the merits of the medicament; he said that its great virtue was that it acted within ten minutes, and that some of his patients had to be careful to be in bed before they took it, because otherwise they fell asleep before they got into bed. My excellent physician, I am afraid, defeated his own ends. His description of the prompt power of his soporific was a challenge to me. I kept myself awake watching very carefully whether the drug really would work in ten minutes or not, and I kept myself awake nearly an hour and a half. To the writer of little moral essays such as these, everything becomes a parable. I could not resist keeping myself awake longer, partly because I began to reflect that it was the role of self-awareness, this watching of the self and what happens to it, that is one of the great distractions, interruptions and, if the phrase be not too strong, curses of the modern world. Some people call it subjectivism, some existentialism—but whatever it is, it is hard to get over it. One watches oneself go to sleep, and thus one does not go to sleep; one watches oneself fall in love, and thus one does not fall in love; one watches oneself writing a paragraph like this, and thus one comes to end it.

Compulsion

Late the other night for no reason at all the line came into my head ". . . the traffic snarl grows worse and worse . . ." and, apparently inevitably, the rhyme "hearse" sprang to mind. I had not been thinking about the traffic problem at all, nor had I any ambition to write a treatise or even a verse on the subject. Yet I found myself composing a verse—to the extent of twenty lines. I do not for a moment pretend that this throws a profound light on the creative process in general, though I suspect poems far more serious got their start in something like the same accidental compulsion of a rhyme.

Our bonds and our necessities turn out often unexpectedly to be our avenues and opportunities. Looking back, we say, "Except for having had to do this, I should never have thought of doing that." An act of creation, even a small act of creation, is a kind of opportunism on a transcendental scale. It is often turning an inconvenience into an occasion, or a persistent inner gnawing and compulsion into what once in a way turns out to seem a felicitous act of invention. All this, pursued far enough, would take us straight into the whole classic controversy of freedom and determinism. The rhyming of "worse" and "hearse" hardly seems like an *adequate* introduction to such a profound theme, but it is an introduction, and only the limits of space—and knowledge—prevent me from developing the theme on a grandiose scale.

The Unendurable Sin

Once when I was eighteen, I complained to a wise elderly friend, aged thirty, that somebody we both knew was an unspeakable bore. He looked at me from the vantage ground of his years, and said knowingly, "By the time you are thirty you will be very grateful if people are no worse than bores." Sometimes now, when I read eloquent passages about the love of all mankind and compassion for everyone, I feel that if I put my heart to it, I could do fairly well with and toward most people; but I cannot help feeling that even the Saints in Heaven must, if they are quite honest with themselves—and of course they would be—confess to a mite of irritation at some of their more long-winded colleagues. It is possible to suffer even fools gladly, but it is not possible to suffer gladly in the presence of a bore. There is a story told of a Chinese sage, bedridden with an incurable illness, who was visited every afternoon at great length by a well-intentioned but extremely dull friend. One afternoon, unable to bear the ennui any longer, the Chinese sage, famous for his exquisite courtesy, said quietly: "Will you please excuse me for a moment while I turn to the wall and draw my last breath?"

These memories and meditations come into my mind because yesterday I experienced what seemed for the time being just such a major calamity. I was riding a bus, and I saw coming down the aisle a heavy-set but, as I knew from many years' experience, a stolidly voluble man, an acquaintance of my family's whom I remembered from my own adolescence. I had scarcely ever been able to answer even civil questions of his with anything better than clearly petulant civility. Now here he was coming down the aisle, and unmistakably recognizing me. The seat beside me was empty. A moment later he was in it.

I had been lecturing that morning on the religious ideal of saintliness, and I had been quite eloquent on the theme of compassion for *all* mankind. I was glad there was none of my students on the bus. Things turned out just as I expected: How was my mother; how was my brother; how was my sister; how was I? Was so-and-so still alive, and was it not too bad about this and that one's death? By the twenty-fifth question, there lay below my brief replies a mounting urge to murder, or just to change my seat.

There is obviously something missing in any possible plan for perpetual peace so long as this sort of bore and boredom go on in the world. I hear somebody whisper, "Well, how about tolerance, if not compassion?" But that is precisely the difficulty. My own threshold of pain—and, I suspect, that of many people—is particularly low when it comes to boredom. My own reserves of tolerance on this head are rapidly exhausted. No civil rights commission is ever going to convince me that bores—not a minority, by the way—have equal rights with everyone else. Some of the classic saints apparently did not mind bores. They felt sometimes, if it is not too irreverent to suggest it, a real kinship with them.

Softer, Kinder, Safer

Softer, kinder, safer! The endearing and insinuating phrase caught my eye one day in the subway—while riding which artery one comes to forget (as one does in cities anyway) that one is under the sky at all. I am not certain what it was that was softer, kinder, safer. I am reasonably clear it was some form of soapsuds, but one has been able to note for a long time now the tender and modulated promise of any number of advertisements which guarantee that things will be smooth, that they will be gentle, that they will be safe. One would think that one was living in the midst of a jungle, where life was marked by the jagged, the violent, and the insecure. To read the advertisements, one would guess that except for the given product advertised, all one's food came to one in rough chunks; that the soap generally available was made of pure grit; and that the ordinary run of toothpastes were likely to explode the moment they were put upon one's toothbrush.

Well, maybe we are living in a jungle. Obviously, primitive man could have felt no more cosmic insecurity than most self-denominated civilized men feel at the present time. Life is comfortable but not soft; it is organized but not smooth; it is ingeniously complicated but not secure. Time was when in a rough world one was invited to escape to some sanctuary or some retreat, but the advertisers have made it easier. One does not even have to move now. The softness, the smoothness, the safety, are brought in packages right into the home. Perhaps in a desperate emergency one will have to walk as far as the nearest drugstore. The telephone is right at hand. When life gets too complicated, all that is necessary is to dial a number and leave a general order for the very best they have in softness, kindness, and safety. And right away, please!

Well, I Doubt It!

I had just handed to my friend's seven-year-old son a copy of Kipling's *Just So Stories*. He looked at the title carefully, read it aloud reflectively. "Just so stories," he repeated with patent reserve. "Well, I doubt it!"

I see in seven-year-old Edward the makings of a literary critic or a rational philosopher. *Just So Stories* indeed! Edward will never be taken in by the apparatus of photographic realism; not Zola nor James Farrell, even, is going, by means of piled-up facts, to persuade him that this is the way, or actually was *la vraie vérité*.

I can, again, see young Edward growing up to be a fine, hard-shelled empirical critic. Theologians had better beware of coming along with grandiose mythologies telling Edward about the origins and destinies of things. Just so, indeed! I should be surprised if Edward went so far as to say, "Well, only just."

I think, on the other hand, books that are frankly fanciful, that pretend to be nothing more than myth or whimsical images or poetic transmutations of life, might win Edward's approval. He is well on the way to keeping a firm distinction in his mind between literal fact and imagination. I suspect a book called *Just As If Stories* would seem to him less questionable. He can understand delightful whoppers, but he does not want all this nonsense about their being true. After all, he has reached the Age of Reason.

Want to See How High I Can Bounce?

My hostess had left the living room for the moment, and her six-year-old daughter Daphne was seated demurely on the divan. She looked at me speculatively for a moment, as if wondering what subject could possibly interest me. Then she said suddenly, quite loudly, and without preamble: "Want to see how high I can bounce?" I promptly admitted a fanatic curiosity, and she bounced quite high and graciously accepted my compliments on her achievement.

Well, I suppose I should not be drawing morals from Daphne's feat. (I should perhaps draw a moral from my own conduct, for her mother, entering the room that moment, said ruefully she had been trying for three months to break Daphne of the habit of bouncing on the expensive and somewhat fragile divan. I made a note that I should never encourage the children of my friends without a visa from their parents.) But doubtless a large motivation of human conduct is summarized in Daphne's exclamation, "Want to see how high I can bounce?" In society, in government, in literature. Never mind that one bounces back down, and that people soon get accustomed to the height of one's bounce and pay no further attention to it. Never mind, either, the virtuosity that goes into our particular kind of bounce—if nobody watches it, a good deal of the spring goes out of the bounce itself. One becomes rather bored with the whole business.

Daphne was annoyed with me when a few minutes

later she asked with the marvelous pertinacity of children, "Want to see how high I can bounce again?" I looked, I am afraid, rather blasé this time. A few minutes later, somewhat diffidently, Daphne asked if I would like to see her new tricycle. Artists need new devices for their audiences. Daphne was learning rapidly the vanity and precariousness of applause. But for the moment, anyway, she had bounced very high.

But You Haven't Changed a Bit

If one has lived long enough, one is sure at irregular intervals to run into old acquaintances who remark in a tone that implies both surprise and enthusiasm, "But you haven't changed a bit." Sometimes there are candid addenda made: "Of course, you have put on a little weight," or "Naturally, you don't look just like the kid you were thirty-five years ago," or, defiantly, "I should have recognized you anywhere." Not only does the acquaintance who says that you have not changed think he is paying a compliment; when one hears such an observation, one is automatically elated. But why?

Does one really have the illusion that in one's youth one was so fine and fair that any change would have been for the worse? Or perhaps the old acquaintance is not merely referring to physical appearance; he is referring to the spiritual and moral tone, the intellectual mode, the nuances of manner—all of which, he insists, have remained identical. And here, too, one finds oneself instinctively and foolishly gratified. Surely it would seem to be a matter for felicitation if one had changed very considerably. Not changed a bit? Indeed! The same enthusiasms, adolescent and uninformed; the identical semi-insights and hasty conclusions, the flashes of what (by eighteen-year-old standards) seemed corruscating wit; the bursts of what (at the same age) passed for lyric ecstasy. A pity if one hadn't improved over all that!

But those who intend a compliment by saying one has

not changed frequently mean the compliment, and are expressing a touching human loyalty to what they earlier knew and liked. In a world where, as Heraclitus remarked early in Greek philosophy, all is changing save the law of change, it is reassuring to find that one's friends are still recognizable, still intrinsically the same. The pleasure is partly that of relieved surprise. The old classmate recognizes the teen-ager in the tycoon, the freshman he once knew in the now formidable public man. The pleasure is half one of pathos—in our hearts we know everything has changed indeed, ourselves and our friends, and when we can clutch at some permanence, discover (or allege to discover) some continuity, we are "arrested, we are rebuked, we are delivered."

Sometimes, it must be confessed however, the hard thought crosses one's mind that there is a note of bitterness or of irony in the phrase, "But you haven't changed a bit." It is not always a compliment that is intended. What is meant is, as an ignorant preacher once eloquently put it: "The leper cannot change his spots."

On Not Keeping a Journal

The journal is become a popular literary mode again. Gide's lifelong personal notebook is coming out in volume after volume, and attracting wide attention. I suspect journals are avidly read by a good many people who rather wish they had kept one, and feel that they can at least settle for some substitute genius who took the trouble to write out his thoughts and his memories. As to Gide, one of the mysteries is where he found time to write anything else *but* his journal. Amiel, of course, hardly did write anything else.

For most of us in the modern world, the energies that might have gone into a journal are drained off in reports to committees, in telephone conversations, in argumentative letters to public utilities. Moreover, it is almost impossible to start to keep a journal without feeling a little self-conscious and perhaps, it must be admitted, a little absurd. In one's mind's eye, one begins to see the five collected volumes. Twenty or thirty years from now in, say, Volume IV, there will be a brief comment: "Saw last night *A Streetcar Named Desire*. Flashes of real insight, genuine characters, but also poetic *langueurs* and considerable rhetoric." In the footnotes, perhaps some conscientious editor will have an explanation next to an asterisk: "A play by a young playwright, Tennessee Williams, well known in the 'forties." And suddenly unquenchable laughter overcomes the incipient five-volume keeper of a journal. Is it really likely that there will be a multi-volumed edition of one's thoughts, and that some editor will devote the dull accolade of footnotes to one's random comments? Perhaps, but it takes an unusually innocent self-confidence to believe it.

Of course, even an uninteresting journal by an uninteresting mind may, forty or fifty years from now, have a documentary value. One can promise oneself perhaps that some critic someday will be saying of one's persistent and insectivorous jottings: "The very commonplaceness of the mind that wrote this journal makes its entries particularly revealing. Here is the average middle-brow intellectual of the period, faithful to all its clichés and naïvely committed to all its current assumptions. If this had been an original mind, it would have been much less interesting to us now than the genteel, well-bred, conventional, and standard type that it is. The poor man thought he was being utterly, uniquely himself. What a perfection of routine banality he really was, and how perfect a mirror of his times! We should be grateful to him that he was not better than he was. Had he been, it would have been much worse for us."

Come to think of it, a journal that is long enough cannot help, in one way or another, being a classic. I am tempted, rather late, to begin now.

Finality Is Where You Find It

It was ten years since I had gone to Europe and I did not need to be reminded that much had happened on both sides of the Atlantic, and on it, since I had last set foot on a transatlantic liner. But things were much as they had been ten years ago, at least on the eve of a voyage. The hundreds of small chores, and what seemed the thousands of little pieces of unfinished business, the letters to be answered, the people to be said good-by to, the dentist to be seen, the shopping to be done, the visits postponed all year that suddenly seemed imperative on the very day before departure. How familiar it all seemed, and how overwhelming.

Well, here it is a few hours later, the pilot long since dropped, the last steamer letter opened. And suddenly, as of old, the visits unmade, the letters unanswered, the ragged edges left ragged—all seem blessedly remote and delightfully negligible. These things will await one's return, or won't: so much the better. And as of old, one turns to this new interim world. There is a reservation to be made for a place in the dining room, a purser's form to be filled out, one's cabin mate to become acquainted with, the passenger list to be conned, the ship to be explored. The world of one's familiar preoccupations is there left behind; the world of Europe is still remote. Sea change, it is called.

And what of those urgencies that one has left behind? There are several ways to write finis to the unfinished.

One way is to leave it quite definitively unfinished. It now hardly seems worth the cost of a radiogram to retrieve or to correct. Five times round the deck makes a mile. The first sitting is at six-thirty, the second at eight. First things first, but the first things of last week are not first any longer. They are, perforce, finished. Finality is where you find it.

Forever Now

My host, a man of letters with a taste for philosophy, and I had been discussing time and eternity on a hilltop by the Mediterranean where indeed it did seem on this summer day as if time must have a stop. Later that day I found myself reflecting on the curious illusion which, it seems to me, has dominated many a reputed thinker from Plato and Plotinus down.

Eternity, in the great mystical and rationalist tradition, as everyone knows, does not mean an endlessly long time. Indeed, no better reason could be sought for an escape from time than the certified prospect that one would, under whatever paradisial circumstances, have to go on living always and endlessly. For time not only bringeth all things—but brings them, the same ones, over and over again: a discovery many people make even before middle age sets in. Immortality that went on endlessly, only in a "world elsewhere," would be as monotonous as if it were perpetuity here in this too-well-explored home cosmos. No, what the great mystics and the great rationalists have meant, is, of course, not a long time but a transtemporal now, an Eternal Now, a present rescued from change, an instant rescued from the flow of time and fixed beyond change or variation in the eternal.

But surely second thought would make it clear that there is precious little to distinguish the Eternal Now of the saint from the passing moment of the secular Epicurean. If eternity is always now, is not the now by which we are completely absorbed, for the time being eternal? A gesture of love, a modulation of music, a stab of pain —are these not of the same dimension, while we are aware of them, as the beatitude of the angels or the tortures of the damned? Everyone has known such moments of Heaven or Hell, instants that were forevers—dreadful or delicious. Doubtless it is from such moments that the mystics have borrowed their notions of eternity. There is little by which one can tell now and forever apart. Now stops only when we forget it, and forever is perhaps only a name for such forgetfulness.

Judgment Day Comes Once an Aeon

These lines are written before the national election, and will appear after it. I have, or ought to have, a feeling, therefore, that much of what I am thinking now or saying now will be quite invalid when the election is over. Certain future widely publicized dates always seem final and decisive. They appear as dividing lines between two epochs, final demarcations of the Era Before and the Era After. It used to amuse schoolboys—it doubtless still does—to imagine somebody dating a letter 51 B.C. *But* even the day after the birth of Christ (if it is not irreverent to say so)—that day itself must have been a very ordinary one in the life of the average citizen of the ancient world. The morning after the burning of Joan of Arc, the routine business of life must have gone on. Afterward usually seems, at least superficially, about the same as did before.

Meanwhile, there are days that mark genuine revolutions in history—days like the birth of Christ or his crucifixion—however little stir they created in their contemporary world. It would be convenient if days that were genuinely decisive could clearly be labeled as such. It would be pleasant, on some golden August morning, to know that this was the beginning of a new age in the world, or on a gray November afternoon, when everything seemed endlessly recurrent, to know that something basically new had happened in our time.

"It is the beginning of the Age of Joy," one might some

morning be informed crisply by the news announcer. "It is reported at Oslo that permanent peace has broken out." One wouldn't believe it, really; one has heard too many days labeled as decisive. This is it, it is said, and it repeatedly is not. It recurrently is not anything.

Whence this habit of looking forward to days of destiny? It is a habit carried over, probably, from childhood, this expectation of *the* crucial day: graduation from grade school, the day one became an Eagle Scout, one's twelfth birthday ("You're a little man now"). But these days come and go, and it is the same world essentially, with the same people in it. History is much less given to crucial days than are school calendars.

It is good for our sense of proportion to become, or to come to know, astronomers. Watchers of the skies live imaginatively among vast times and distances; the crises they note are millions of years apart; only once in a very great human while do they discover a comet or a planet. The Day of Judgment does not come every day, however much the Angel Gabriel, as in Marc Connolly's *The Green Pastures,* sits eagerly polishing up his horn.

(1948)

Au Petit Bonheur

Doubtless certain expressions in a foreign language, even ones quite familiar, or erroneously understood, have a freshness and pathos that they cannot possibly have to their native user. I am confident that no Frenchman would or could have had quite the same feeling that I had when I recently saw in France—over a little shop selling miscellaneous gifts and souvenirs—the sign "Au Petit Bonheur." Certainly the meditation it induced had little to do with the costume jewelry, the pocketbooks, the cigarette lighters, on display to catch the pennies of tourists in the Riviera resort village, nor with the true meaning of the phrase, which is "bargain," not "happiness."

How suggestive an expression, I found myself thinking. The little happiness, the minor felicity, the modest joy. . . . Moralists are always talking of the grand and comprehensive happiness. Even Aristotle insists that happiness can be conceived of only in the long view, and perhaps cannot be attributed safely to anyone until his life is over. The poets, too, when they speak of felicity, usually think of it in grandiose terms. It is a beatitude, it is eternal, it is Heaven—or near it. And to the romantic imagination, joy is always conceived of as a great joy, an altitude, an ecstasy, a forever.

Well, the way things are going in the world—the way, one might say, that they have always gone—it might be well to settle for the small happiness, the little joy. I think Montaigne would have been on my side, and Epicurus and Ecclesiastes—the last-named because he was quite despairing of any long or large felicity. The French have always specialized in the *petit bonheur:* the small omelette, the little wine, the intimate foyer of enjoyment. The English have celebrated it, too. Austin Dobson was one of the prophets of this moderate aspiration:

> Here in this sequestered close
> Bloom the hyacinth and rose.

Rupert Brooke, homesick for Grantchester, the tranquil village near Cambridge, asked:

> Stands the church clock at ten to three?
> And is there honey still for tea?

And the small pleasures that make a tempered happiness persisted in an older Germany, long after that unhappy land had gone in for bigness and empire.

Is it sour grapes to settle for the little happiness: to aim to make happiness out of the most modest ingredients: little things lovingly collected, simple meals in modest surroundings with unpretentious friends, discoursing, perhaps, on not too grand ideas? Is the little happiness cherishable only because, as one grows older, neither private ecstasy nor public utopias seem any longer feasible? Do we tell ourselves the unspectacular moments satisfy only because all moments are threatened, because even gentle goods—like honey for tea in England—cannot be taken for granted any longer? How many millions in the world would now compound for the *petit bonheur!* Included among those millions, no doubt, the readers of this meditation—and its author.

Sincerity As a Fine Art

I remember often during my early adolescence listening to older people making conversation. I vowed I would never willingly be a conspirator at such transparent hypocrisies. When *I* went out to dinner, I found myself saying, I should speak only when I felt like it, and I should say only what was on my mind. I used to listen while my elders pretended to have a fascinated interest in visitors with whom I knew they had only the most remote concern, and hear them discuss with affected animation matters that I knew bored them to pain. I remember having had it explained to me that this was the least that good manners demanded. It was at this moment that I came to the conclusion that good manners and dubious morals had much in common.

In these matters, I have become subdued to the general color of civilized society. It has long ago been brought home to me that a guest has obligations in addition to that of eating the food provided by his host. It is fair enough that one should, if not sing, at least converse for one's supper. I have even come to believe that my elders of long ago were more interested in their visitors than I had supposed. I have lighted upon the fact that questions asked out of politeness may elicit answers that are fascinating on their own. An enchanting story may be the unearned increment of a conventional inquiry.

And yet I have not ceased to be troubled at the momentum with which on a social occasion one is embarked on a brief career of insincerity. I have found myself expressing opinions on Russia or on psychiatry that I had not known I possessed. I have sometimes, out of sheer inability to get out of it, maintained a position on old-age security, or on old age itself, that, save for some impulsive remark I had let fall, I should not have considered it a point of honor to defend as my considered philosophy on the subject. On shamefully numerous occasions, I have repeated an anecdote by which I was myself bored to death. I have talked with dowagers about literature, art, and education, at moments when all three of these lofty themes seemed to me insufferably tedious and stuffy.

I have come to admire those sturdy individualists who say—as I once planned to say—only whatever comes into their minds, and speak only when they are spoken to, and perhaps not even then. But I must admit I find them difficult socially, these high-minded boors who can be pricked into only the most minimal of replies, these dedicated roughnecks who find a savage pleasure in telling you without compromise what they think of everything, including your loyalties and your enthusiasms—and possibly yourself.

There must be some way of acting both agreeably and sincerely. It is a fine art, practiced, one is told, by a few witty eighteenth-century courtiers. But wits today are rather celebrated for their malignity. It is a difficult alternative, that between truth and charm, and I confess that I am tempted to seek the easier and more genial path. If one plumped for sincerity, one would get to be

known simply as a bear, a bear who would soon be walking alone, a boorish bear who at any rate would seldom
be invited out to dinner. As Santayana remarks somewhere, "For a man of sluggish mind and bad manners,
there is decidedly no place like home."

First They Suffer, Then They Sing

"Great art can come only from suffering," said the eminent art dealer, as he lit his cigar after the sumptuous lunch in the home of our wealthy and connoisseur host. He was a man of taste as well as shrewdness, and he knew a good deal about the value of a work of art, as well as its price. He had been, I had been told, something of a romantic poet in his youth, and at sixty he still looked the after-image of the part, a thin, "spiritual," finely cut face, a slim body, meditative eyes, delicate hands.

"Don't *you* think that all great art must come from suffering?" he asked, turning to me, who was sitting on the drawing-room couch beside him.

"No, I don't," I said. "I think that's a conventional sentimental illusion."

"Ah, no," the art dealer sighed, "it isn't. Take Michelangelo, take Dante, take Beethoven, take El Greco, take Keats, take Baudelaire, take Rimbaud."

"Hold on!" I said. "Take—" . . . and then I could not think of my happy artist in any era of any of the arts.

"You see," said the art dealer.

"Oh, but yes I can," I said triumphantly. "Benevenuto Cellini. He seemed to do all right, and to feel he was doing all right, and if you will give me time I'll think of some others."

"I don't think you'll find any," said the art dealer. "Remember, even when an artist seems happy in terms of external conditions, there is an inner misery." He put his hand on his heart. "One never knows. Often an artist completely conceals his suffering from the world, but it is privately there. Abolish misery, and I promise you art will disappear."

"Yes," I said, putting as much irony into my tone as I could, "there is something in what you say. And if there is, I think several important things follow. We must give up all improvement of the condition of the poor. We can't afford to lose the chance of developing some first-rate poverty-stricken artists. It's going to be pretty difficult, with old-age security and all that; it's up to the government to arrange that a few chosen, gifted persons each year be made to do without adequate shelter or leisure or food. We must see that their families are half-starving, and, if possible, give the artist an incurable, or, at the very least, a painful, disease. Even if we allow him to be healthy and comfortable, and perhaps even give him a little time for his work, we must be sure he does not go to a psychiatrist to be cured of his inward miseries. We must keep him from marrying if he is in love, possibly by arranging that his love be unrequited, or by doping him up so that he cannot fall in love at all, and is therefore still more miserable. We must make it impossible for him to obtain a divorce if he is unhappily married. We must teach his children to be unfilial, and alienate from him all his friends. We must not allow him a moment of pure joy."

"I should not go quite that far," said the art dealer, a

little taken aback by what he took to be my sudden con-
version, "but you get my point. For the present there is
still enough misery in the world without the necessity of
its being arranged by the state."

"Good!" I said. "Then art is safe for a little while."

Distressed Merchandise

Recently a wine dealer recommended to me as a gift a fine Burgundy of "one of the great years." He sang its praises with the lyric exactitude of the expert, and then astonished me by quoting a fantastically low price.

"Why," I asked, "if this wine is as distinguished as you say, is its price so ordinary—in fact, rather less than ordinary?"

"Oh," he said promptly, "this is distressed merchandise!"

The term was new to me, and he explained it. A shipper or a middleman short of money will unload even some prized wares at a sacrifice, and these notable goods then become classified as distressed merchandise.

The term has pleasantly preoccupied my reflections from time to time ever since. As I read the weekly journals, the little reviews, and the little pamphlets of ideas expanded into books, the epithet "distressed merchandise" seems to me a convenient and transferable one. There is evidence that there are authors and thinkers who have hastily sold out good ideas, often sloppily packaged, under the pressures of time, and occasionally even under the pressures of money.

In the current scene of political action and political morals, there are instances of distressed merchandise too —high ideals that have been auctioned off cheap; principles that have been sold for a song; political moralities of the first water that have been got rid of over the counter. Some dedication that came to maturity in a "great year" is exchanged for a quick expediency in a poor one.

But sometimes the current intellectual merchandise is distressed in another sense, and distressing as well. How much we are hearing these days about "anxiety"—as if it were almost a desirable principle of the actions or of the corruption of man, as if it were something to cling to—and the "absurd," as if it were the central fact of existence. The bookshops, too, are full of unhappy commodities. But they differ from the wares recommended by my wine dealer. They do not come from the sunny side of the hill, they are not of a great year, nor do they go cheap.

Aristides the Sensible

As schoolboys we all learned about Aristides the Just. He was so celebrated for his justice that his very name became tiresome as well as suspicious. It is hard to know whether he was more resented for being just, or more suspect for being thought to be. There is a different kind of Aristides whom surely I am not the only one to find oppressive—Aristides the Sensible.

I have never actually met him, but I have friends who are constantly speaking of him. He is invariably sensible, equable, reasonable, sane. He is subject to no excess of passion or prejudice; there is no "if," as in Kipling, about his keeping his head when all about him are losing theirs. In the midst of crises, his own or those of the world, he maintains an exquisite calmness and admirable serenity.

Let some wild wind of political doctrine sweep across the country: he remains steadfast. Let some mode of philosophical excess or literary exaggeration become current: with quiet good sense, he estimates it exactly, and with courtesy and reserve sees through it and sees around it. When pessimists foresee the organized self-extinction of the human race by atomic energy, he reminds one of long perspectives and of astronomical vistas. When enthusiasts see some imminent Utopia, he always inserts a realistic reminder of the actual and a warning as to the limits of the possible.

I know it should be exhilarating even to hear about such a calm paragon of good sense, but the more I hear of Aristides the Sensible, the more I find him impossible. If only he would go mildly mad occasionally, or once burst into nonsense. If only once I could hear that he had lapsed into hysteria, or displayed even the slightest eccentricity. It stands to reason that one should admire a thoroughly reasonable man, but even hearing about him raises my blood pressure. His mere existence is a smug and invidious comment on the rest of us. If I ever meet him, and my friends are always promising to introduce us, I shall be tempted to revise the old English verse and say to him:

> I do not like you, Dr. Fell.
> The reason is not hard to tell:
> You practice reason far too well.
> I do not like you, Dr. Fell.

Dance Without Music

The theory of business cycles seems fairly well established in economics, but there are cycles too in the business of the arts. There was the announcement just the other day of a ballet without music where, the director announced, the participants were trained to dance not by the beating of time heard but by the geometry of design seen. Dialectically, even practically, it is possible, I suppose, to distinguish choreography from the music which accompanies it. But one's tastes harden, like one's arteries, and for myself a ballet with music seems to me more attractive than one without it.

Nonetheless, it is a temptation to let the mind roam over analogous possibilities. I would enjoy an exhibition of painting not only without subject matter but without color and without composition. Come to think of it, I have sometimes run across such things, though they are not announced as such. It would be extraordinarily interesting to go to a concert where the music had no chords, no melody, and no rhythm, or to read poetry without euphony, without meter, without image. Sometimes I think these singular pleasures have been afforded of late in the galleries, bookshops, and museums.

All this I know is perverse or unfair. The pictorial design of the dance, I do not need to be informed, is distinct from that of the musical accompaniment. But just the same, how nice it is to loll back into the comfortable convention of ballet with music, of painting with line and color, of poetry with melody, rhythm, and image. There are moments when one enjoys seeing what can be "done without" in a given art. But such astringent and heroic explorations are on the whole less fun than they might be. I look forward sometime—say, next week—to going to an old-fashioned—shall we say, horse-and-buggy—ballet, that uses the cumbrous and probably gratuitous apparatus of lovely sound, in addition to the loveliness of bodies in motion. It is sheer aesthetic laziness, I know, but then one does not turn to the arts primarily to see how much one can do without. There are other opportunities for such austerities and asceticisms.

On Counting Worlds

A few years ago—and how long it seems—the phrase "one world" was on everybody's tongue, and the hope of one world was in everybody's heart. Now, more soberly and ominously, the phrase has become "two worlds." We are told, not without evidence, that they are irreconcilable, and the possibility of the world becoming one has been declared for the long tragic present an irrelevant dream.

If the whirling planet could speak, it might quietly remind those crawling about its surface or flying above it that it really is still one world which (as Gilbert reminded us in the *Bab Ballads*) rolls on.

But if some impatient reader reminds me that, of course, by one world is meant not the physical planet but the human scene, and that that human scene is now, as we are credibly informed, two worlds, then two worlds are almost as much of a mess as one. There are of course numberless worlds, often very small ones, that hardly have a speaking acquaintance with one. Five minutes across the park from Columbia University is the teeming world of Negro Harlem. Ten minutes away are Spanish-speaking slums. Two minutes away from Philosophy Hall is a building devoted to Law, and another to Business. Pluriverse, as James once said, would be a better name for what we live in.

It would be fine if we could have one world. Or would it? In too many senses, we are already having it. Airplanes transport us with the utmost rapidity to distant places that are becoming so much like home that we might just as well have stayed home. International radio networks can mutually broadcast recognizable mediocrity if the world really becomes one. In the sense of a vast undifferentiated standard of dullness, we might be glad to abandon the phrase and the idea altogether. Perhaps what we really mean is simply the fact recognized long ago by the ancient Stoics—that we are, in the possibility of reason and in the identity of our fate, brothers. Perhaps what we really want is a universal chance for as many worlds as possible. One world, even two worlds, is after all a very small number. It does not need astronomers to remind us how many worlds there are, including these desiring or dreaming ones within all of us into which, in dream and in wish, we retire.

One Less Bother

"I am quite sure you would not be interested in it at all," said a friend, speaking of a novel about which I had expressed some curiosity. "It's no good at all, and it is not the kind of book in which you would in any case have the least pleasure."

I respected my friend's judgment of writing, and I knew he was very accurate in divining my tastes. "Well, then, that's that," I said to myself. "One less book to promise myself to read."

I have a perverse pleasure, that must be shared by many—the delight of release from the additional obligations imposed by announced new masterpieces, paintings that one must see, music that one must hear, novels that one must read, plays that one must attend, conferences that one must take part in. I make rather a cult of reading the daily reviews of books and plays and music, and checking off with delight those that begin in effect: "One wonders what on earth prompted anyone to write or to publish . . ." or "Why Conductor X selected this current Italian bit of musical chaos is not clear . . ." or "There must doubtless be some who are moved by this tawdry and dull melodrama produced last night." I bless the writers of such devastating pronouncements. They have given me an alibi for reading old books (since there are clearly no good new ones), or chatting with friends, or doing nothing at all, or writing something like this.

Back from Nature

Only the city-bred could possibly feel that after a spell in the country they were returning to life by returning to town. But autumn after autumn there must be thousands who feel, as I do, that it may be all very well about trees and grass and wind and rain, but it's very comforting to get back from the nuisance of fires to steam heat, from fields and streams to streets and busses. Time and again there have been back-to-nature movements—in life, in literature, and in art. But the revolts not least interesting are those away from nature—to formalism in art, to urbanization and urbanity in life, to the sophisticated in manners, to the disciplined in action; from the spontaneities of progressive education, freedom once more shuddering into rules. I suspect we're in the midst of one of these back-from-nature movements now. The words discipline and order rear their formal-looking heads. Even the farm imitates and embodies the streamlining of cities. Some have gone so far back from nature that they are in the realm of Non-Being, itself. In a world where there is, as atomic scientists assure us, no place to hide, Non-Being would seem a good place to get back to. I expect shortly a Back-to-Nothingness movement (about as far from nature as one could get), quietude and peace at last!

On Being Non-Omniscient

The night the Russian radio announced the change from Molotov to Vishinsky as Foreign Minister, I was listening to one of the best of the news commentators. After repeating the facts and speculating for five minutes on the various early interpretations of the meaning of the announcement, he said unexpectedly and refreshingly, "I don't know any more about it than I have already told you"—which, as he seemed clearly to recognize, was not very much. I suspect it would not be very difficult for a speaker or a writer rapidly to acquire a world-wide reputation merely by an honest and candid avowal of his ignorance, or the limitations of his knowledge, concerning the tangled strands of events in the contemporary world.

The habit of ominscience, the inner feeling of certainty, grows of necessity in the professional speaker or teacher or writer. To paraphrase Santayana's comment on teaching, "In the presence of a hundred youthful up-turned faces a man can scarcely refrain from saying more than he knows." But the temptation to be apodictic and all-knowing grows even more, I suspect, among those who have to comment daily in print or over the air on the tragic and urgent events of our day. There is a subtle compulsion to lay down the law and extrapolate the meaning.

A writer or speaker cannot help knowing that in a time of confusion his professional stock in trade is certainty. The public does not turn to a columnist or a commentator to find simply a mirror of its own doubts and confusions. People listen and read because they hope to have those doubts resolved. If they find a writer or a speaker who provides them with a set of clear dogmas that utter their deepest hopes or fears, they feel they have acquired wisdom. But even those who have found one voice to follow, occasionally by accident hear other and contradictory voices. They learn after a while that there are various brands of omniscience whose claims conflict with each other. They become disillusioned; there arises in their minds the suspicion that no one knows much more than they do and that no one can speak with authority. A man might thus become known, if for nothing else, for his disarming candor, by announcing, as the commentator did, that he didn't really know. It may be recalled that Socrates regarded as his one claim to wisdom his realization that he was the only man in Athens who knew he didn't know. But of course posterity refuses to take him seriously. Socratic irony, we call it.

Theory of Knowledge

I listened with interest to the visiting philosopher who was reading a paper on some of the problems of knowledge. The ones he was preoccupied with were those familiar enough to professional students of epistemology and strange enough to the undebauched outsider. The visitor was concerned with the validity of perceptions as media of our knowledge of the external world. He was arguing against sense data and for a theory of "appearing." Needless to say, he found himself soon in the midst of numerous paradoxes—metaphysical paradoxes, he called them—in view of the fact that if something appears, there must be something to do the appearing. That unacknowledged philosopher, Winnie the Pooh, at a certain point in his saga, says, "I hear a buzz. When there is a buzz there must be something to do the buzzing and the only thing that can buzz like that is a bee." Winnie the Pooh was obviously beginning a long career in epistemology.

But hoary as is the tradition of the theory of knowledge, and uncertain as is the status of perception, I could not help reflecting, as I listened to the paper, how singular it is that philosophers should so long have selected this particular theme when they begin to talk of "knowledge."

How fantastic it is that human beings should have made a problem of the mere possibility of relationship between the self and the world—between private consciousness and public objects. Without brushing aside the real issues that arise in reflection on knowledge, I could not refrain from thinking of those moments, half-disturbing and half-revealing, when human beings in a sudden access of what seems clarity and vision say to themselves: "Now I know!"

At some unexpected passage in conversation, a friend one has known familiarly for years, by an inadvertent phrase or a casual gesture, suddenly lights himself up for us. I leave to students of psychoanalysis and Gestalt psychology the long processes of subconscious maturation, the unsuspected movement toward what, when it comes, is a sudden "Eureka," the surprised (though not always delightful) sense of discovery of coherence or meaning. At certain moments usually connected with art or love or friendship, what has been "seen as in a glass darkly" is seen now "face to face."

There may be all sorts of explanations of this certitude, of the natural history of this authenticity which often without premonition accompanies moments of passion, creation, or enjoyment. But any theory of knowledge that presumes to deal with human awareness must deal with these things as well as with "the reality of the external world." There is more awareness of Heaven and earth than is dreamed of in routine epistemology, or than can be accounted for by the usual vocabulary of perceptions, sense data, and inference. The problem of knowing all of a sudden, of clarity all of a heap, needs to be added to the more conventional puzzles of knowledge. The heart has its knowledge that knowledge does not know.

The Novelty of the Old-Fashioned Virtues

Only a few years ago, a novel revolving around the theme of loyalty would have seemed dated and old-hat. Galsworthy's play *Loyalties* seemed a little old-fashioned even a generation ago, and it is a long time since Royce's "Philosophy of Loyalty" and his idea of "loyalty to loyalty" have had any vogue. But the fact of treason in wartime, and the accusations of treason in the postwar world, have made this recently old-fashioned virtue suddenly acutely modern again.

In the same way, there was a time not so long ago when all one had to do was to recite the Victorian cliché, "I was born of poor but honest parents," to draw a laugh. "Honesty is the best policy" was a copybook maxim that one would hesitate to quote seriously. But now in a world given over to conflicting propagandas, at a time when the big and the little lie have become instruments of public policy in many parts of the world, honesty has again become a virtue of crucial timeliness and obvious necessity.

Thus, likewise, it had become the fashion in the 'twenties to laugh out loud at asceticism, and to hoot at chastity. Who would have predicted that a generation later a novel like Somerset Maugham's *The Razor's Edge,* whether by intention or not, a propaganda for the unworldly life, should have millions of readers? And who, incidentally, would have thought that in an age of notorious skepticism there should have been so many books celebrating the simple virtues of faith and of devotion? There are all sorts of moral lessons to be drawn from these phenomena, and I leave it to the reader to draw any ones he pleases. The one I should like to draw is the relativity of the old-fashioned and the up-to-date in human feeling, the parochialism of any moment of time. Old-fashioned virtues indeed! Loyalty, honesty, chastity, faith—these seem to be the *avant garde* of virtues of the present hour, and the preoccupations of leading articles in all the little reviews.

Valley of the Shadow

Everyone recalls as a child or in youth saying with heartfelt sincerity: "I will remember this the rest of my life," or "I shall treasure this always," or "I shall read books till the day I die." "The rest of one's life," "always," "till the day I die": there was a good deal of emotional capital invested in those terms, for those terms meant an infinite perspective. To the young, "always" seems a very long time indeed, and "the rest of one's life," when one is young, is an endlessly long stretch. "Till the day I die" seems, though even the young know better, to be eternity.

These reflections occurred to me the other day when a friend claimed to be depressed by the imminence of his fiftieth birthday. He was somber with thoughts of mortality, and I tried to cheer him. I reminded him of how, at the age of fifty, the passions presumably were less pressing, the agitations of ambition less compulsive. One had learned to cultivate one's garden or to tend one's tropical fish. Even the major anxieties of the world one could face with prospective detachment, and the major hopes of the world with the generosity of a mind looking beyond one's own day and one's own involvement.

My friend had thought of all those cool comforts. But he reminded me of a few things too, less comforting. It was too late by now even to consider further the major projects still unbegun. The postponements one had extravagantly repeated from year to year were not so expendable any more. The vista of infinite alternatives was by now narrowed; the choices were fewer, and each one made was more clearly final. The languages one had not learned, the countries one had not visited—there were still many of those, and one could not learn all tongues, explore all lands. What was more, he pointed out, the desire of choosing itself vanished with each successive postponement.

"And there are other things you have forgotten," he said. "Under fifty, I had the foolish feeling of being the contemporary of everyone except the very old. I could talk without a sense of barrier to anyone between twenty-five and fifty. I fancied until very recently that even the very young regarded me as their chronological equal. But I don't any more. I look across the chasm of the years to those who do not recall President Wilson, or Roosevelt in his first term, or the beginning of radio and the sound movies, or the time when Freud and Joyce were novelties, and Rockefeller Center a blueprint. Moreover, older people with whom I have gradually come to feel at home are suddenly quitting this world. The obituary pages are filled with the names of my friends, and babies are being born who will not believe I ever could have been young. And I leave out," he said, "the increasing physical disabilities."

"Look here," I said, "you exaggerate. Just wait a while; wait," I said with the portentousness of one who has already entered the valley of the shadow, "until you are fifty-two!"

"To the Layman—"

"To the layman—" How often the phrase has put us in our place, all of us! For there are very few of us who are not laymen, about everything except a small specialty. Sometimes we are called the general public, or the general reader, or the common man. But whatever the name given us, it is meant as a condescension. The layman is the one for whom technicalities are translated, who judges ineptly as far as he can judge at all in matters vastly beyond his comprehension. The layman may be a lawyer, doctor, engineer, Sanskrit scholar, or expert on Etruscan inscriptions. But he is a layman all the same, about everything that lies outside of engineering, medicine, Sanskrit, or Etruscan.

Well, we are all laymen together, absurdly and humiliatingly innocent of everything but our own narrow specialties. It rather sets one up, as a matter of fact, to think that with respect to the incidence of taxation, Einstein knows not a whit more than one does oneself, and that André Gide is as ignorant as you or I on the present state of cancer research—that the Pope himself is infallible only in questions of faith and morals, but likely to make mistakes in English, or in subtraction, or in the understanding of nuclear fission. It helps one's morale to think that ultimately all questions of public policy are addressed to each of us in his capacity of layman.

It is we laymen who ultimately have to understand the world and get the hang of it. Without us (for we are the vast majority) ultimate decisions cannot be made or carried out. It is we who meet at dinner parties and in busses, who sit next to one another on trains and planes, and wait in queues for tickets at box offices.

To paraphrase Lincoln, God must have loved laymen, he made so many of them. It is not the poets, as the Irish poet O'Shaughnessy suggested, but we laymen who are "the movers and shakers of the world forever, it seems." Perhaps it is our slow inability to understand too easily and too much that keeps the world from being moved about too rapidly or too drastically. Compared with us, experts seem, except in trivial matters, ignorant, and specialists extremely narrow.

Goethe—Mephistopheles Speaking

By the time these lines appear, the Goethe celebrations will have quieted down a little, all the speeches will have been made, all the anthologies published, and all the lessons drawn for our time from Goethe's wisdom. The mountains of Colorado will cease to resound with praises of that great Germanic Greek, that great First European, that great lover, that great romantic, that comprehensive sage.

It is not to be expected that we should feel at home equally with all the Olympians. One is entitled to one's choices. One is also entitled to one's allergies. Goethe, or the Goethe legend, has for a long time now been one of mine. There is a Mephistopheles in all of us—not simply in *Faust*—and I find the denying devil in me active about Goethe. A curious kind of stuffiness has, for me, come to be associated with his name, despite the exquisite lyrics, the moving quality of parts of *Faust*, the perceptiveness of *Poetry and Truth*. But, insofar as I have discovered a philosophy in Goethe, I have not liked it. It has always seemed to me adolescent, promoted out of all conscience into a grandiose *Weltanschauung*. Experience, experience! And nothing to be learned from any of it, save that there is to be a new experience that will transcend anything yet experienced. Then, too, Goethe was so infuriatingly successful—as lover, as sage, as literary dictator.

It was a great pleasure to me to discover in a volume of

Goethe's miscellaneous writings a letter he wrote in English at the age of sixteen largely for the exercise. It is comforting to think that at sixteen one could have done no worse in German. That letter gave another dimension to Goethe, humor, but the humor was not intended. Goethe puts me in the mood for Heine. I can hardly wait for an anniversary of Heine. The Goethe year, God be praised, is nearly over. *"Ueber allen Gipfeln ist Ruh"* even in Aspen, Colorado, where Goethe's praises have been sung by a whole bevy of contemporary eminences. How lovely is the silence. *"Verweile doch! du bist so schoen."* That's what a year-long celebration does for one. It creates an antibody of feeling against the very hero it was designed to celebrate.

(1949)

Conversation Piece

A wire recorder is surely one of the most bemusing gadgets to enter the home of modern man. It is, for one thing, a mildly malicious plaything. It is an irresistible temptation to have a group of friends engage in conversation, on some high or some mighty theme, and a few moments later play back to them the exact record of their comments, with all the uh's and ah's, all the dogmatisms and solecisms, all the casual revelations of prejudice, the nonsequiturs and banality, left in. If it be said that this is not quite playing fair, the answer is that the one playing the trick is himself included in any such recording, and his defects are played back as ruthlessly as those of his victims. Even when a friend knows he is being recorded, the results are always, in one respect at least, surprising. To no one, of course, does his own voice ever sound like himself. It is always pitched too high or too low, it is always too husky or too shrill, too rough or too smooth. Everyone else's voice sounds perfectly natural.

What is most amazing to those who listen is what a conversation sounds like a few minutes after it has been held. How many sentences only barely get started, how few ever come to a coherent end! How many crosscurrents of themes and ideas!—even though many motifs crop up with a certain symmetry, so that even the most random conversation has an unexpected loose order and progression of its own.

But how dull an epigram sounds a second time, how

outrageous and flat a repeated and expected pun! How glad everyone is to be informed that the recorded conversation can be promptly and completely "erased" by some magical-seeming magnetic rearranging of molecules. It is a relief to everyone to know that the recorder is turned off, and that one's shafts and sallies, one's ragged grammar and wretched bleatings, have no more certain immortality than the vanishing memories of those present. And, one reflects, what a blessing it is that even the most naturalistic novelist does not record quite what people say. What a bore literature would be were it as faithful as a wire recorder!

And Gladly Serve

It is the natural expectation of anyone called to serve on a jury that he will be asked to serve in a case involving, at the very least, treason. A murder case would, of course, be delightful, if it were not that one might, in voting guilty, have to be a party to meting out capital punishment. The luck of nearly everyone I know has been to be a juror in a petty civil action involving no great sums and no great issues. Well, no great sums. But I could not help noting, somewhat awed, in the course of the petty legal action in which I was involved as a juror, as the piddling testimony progressed, that there *were* great issues involved, all the principles of morality, of law, and of justice. I could feel in the close attentiveness of my fellow jurors that they thought so too.

And what an education in nice distinctions we jurors were having—between the relevant and the irrelevant, between points of fact and points of law, between what was the recounting of a fact and what the retailing of an opinion on the part of a witness. How fine it is, I kept secretly murmuring to myself, that in the Anglo-Saxon tradition a group of ordinary citizens like us here in the box are called upon to decide a case involving these nice points and these ultimate values. How nobly and clearly the conscientious judge instructs us, helps us see what is material and what is immaterial. How well-protected are everything and the rights of everybody. For two days we followed the case closely; all of us carefully obeyed the

167

judge's instructions not to discuss the case with our fellow jurors nor with anyone else during the recess. At the end of two days we were all ready conscientiously to decide the issue, and the thin-lipped lady who had often served on juries before was obviously going to take her line, whatever it was, and hold to it. The case involved alleged fraud, and it would be wonderful to have a chance to ask the judge to define what was faith, what was fraud, in this world. I began to feel as if I were one of Socrates' jurors deciding on the fate, not of thirty-six hundred dollars, but of life and death itself, the life and death of justice.

It was somewhat of an anticlimax to have the judge decide after a half-hour's private consultation with the lawyers on both sides that the thing indicated was a directed verdict, which the foreman of the jury repeated after the judge. It was a bitter pill not to have a chance to decide what was right and wrong, and yet rather a relief. It is difficult enough in one's own life to have to decide for oneself. The jury system is all very well, I reflected, and a fine democratic institution, but how convenient to have official omniscience to turn to, how relaxing to turn to a certified judge for judgment.

Fellow Traveler—Old Meaning

It is now almost impossible to use the word "fellow traveler" in its older and face sense. There was a time, only yesterday, when the epithet conjured up tablemates on a ship, companions in a club car, seat-mates in a bus in Devon or Colorado. Fellow travelers, almost by definition, were amiable or, at any rate, picturesque. They were, say, passengers in the compartment in an Irish train, full of voluble friendliness. They were the young soldiers just back from Guam, or en route to Texas, beside one in the smoking car. To think of oneself as a fellow traveler was not to think of oneself as an innocent or sinister conniver at revolution, as a liberal who, knowing or unknowing, was a Communist front.

In the traditional sense, a fellow traveler might be anything professionally. But for the time being, both you and he stood to each other only in the relation of passengers on the same vehicle, riders to the same destination, or to destinations on the same road. Thus one recalls years later how one shared a cabin on a steamer with a missionary en route to Africa, an engineer on his way to Siam. For the interval, one shared the same meals and the same storms, and the same little cosmos of other passengers, on deck and in the lounge.

Fellow traveling used to be half the fun of travel. But, as many have observed, it is curiously lacking in air travel. Passengers are strangely uncommunicative in an airplane. Partly, it is that conversation is limited to one's neighbor. But, also, most passengers regard an airplane as simply a speedy way of getting there, a fast box to be transported in. The sooner it is over, the better. The very time one spends in the plane is begrudged. As well get into a long conversation with strangers in an elevator in Rockefeller Center as to talk to a neighbor in a plane.

But there is, I think, a subtler reason for silence aloft. Even those who are not frightened in planes are subtly aware it is an unwonted place for people to be. The earthbound human feels it abnormal to be in the air. Insecurity and transitoriness explain why plane passengers are so psychologically isolated, each from the others. Each man is an airborne island. For the fellowship of travel is impossible at three hundred miles an hour and in the stratosphere. "Fellow traveler" might as well be given over to grim political uses. In an air age one travels alone.

Remote from Where?

Everyone, I suppose, knows the story of the Boston boy who, over lunch in Harvard Square, remarked to the Kansas boy that Kansas was far away. "Far from where?" was the sturdy Midwestern reply. I thought of the story one summer when I was living on a small ranch in Wyoming. We were forty miles from the nearest telegraph office, ten miles from the nearest telephone, two hundred miles from the nearest railroad to the East, the center of my universe. Mails seemed oddly slow. They came every day on an R. F. D. route but, because of difficult connections, even airmail from New York took anywhere from three to four days.

"Well, you have made yourself inaccessible," one friend wrote, though whether he was merely noting the fact or complaining about it I could not determine. It was out of the world, I wrote to my friend, delightfully remote. But within a few days I found myself wondering—remote from where, remote from what? The papers arriving late did, it seemed, carry news that was remote from me. In vast metropolitan centers, one is no nearer great events than when one is in Wyoming. Actually, if, as some think, the decisive events of the future are being shaped in China, here I was two thousand miles nearer Shanghai than I would have been in New York. Remote from the world of society, fashion, and power? Most of us are remote from those in New York. Removed from one's immediate obligations and responsibilities? In a way, yes

—from friends, yes. But how much more clear and near some of these seemed, seen in the perspective of imagination in this lucid altitudinous light. And as for oneself, how much closer one seemed to oneself, one's private and authentic being, without the distractions of the telephone and telegram and frequent mail. By the end of the summer, I decided that remote meant remote from these pines, from those cleanly lined mountain peaks, from this transparent air. Here, one was distant simply from the circumference of life, and a little nearer oneself. What was it Shelley said about poetry, the center and circumference of knowledge? Here in this silence, among the pines and aspen, one felt one was at the center chiefly.

As I Was Saying

The other night, in his car, a friend began a story. Something in the traffic interrupted him, and somehow, as I happened later to realize, he never took up the thread or began again. None of us, including the interrupted friend, seemed to have noticed that something had begun and not ended. "Not worth repeating now," he said when I reminded him.

Life, William James said, is a series of interruptions. It is a little depressing sometimes to think how much is left unfinished business, unachieved pleasure, stories of which we do not hear the end, friendships begun in summer leisure but never later picked up. As one thinks about it, one's life seems strewn with projects left hanging in mid-air, enterprises abandoned, affections diminished or lost by distance or by default. And in affairs not concerning oneself, time seems filled with unfinished stories. People bob into prominence and vanish, reputations sizzle into climax and sputter out. Once in Brazil I ran quite unexpectedly into a character who had been the center of a great literary scandal twenty-five years ago. By accident I saw what had happened to that story. Well, I doubt whether we want all stories ended. One of our fears is that the story itself will come to an end, and we do not bless the astronomers who assure us they know the end of the cosmic saga, in which all the myths and legends of civilization will come to an end forever, and there will be a vast frozen silence. But in that silence, perhaps, there will eventually be a stir of life, saying, as it were, "As I was saying." And if on a smaller time scale we worry, as many of us fairly continually do, that our civilization at last will end, even if the solar system will not yet, we may console ourselves that something in it will survive. Art, religion, and philosophy will in time take up the story again. Another age will have forgotten even that there had been an interruption, and will hear the spirit of man murmur once more, "As I was saying . . ."

One Can't Have Everything

"One can't have everything," I replied to my friend who complained that he would like to live in the Virgin Islands, were it not that he couldn't see paintings and hear opera there.

"Why not?" he asked. "I mean, why not morally? I have been told," and his voice grew a little irritable, "ever since I was a small child, that one can't have everything. One can't have one's cake and eat it too. One can't have the best of both worlds; one can't be both horse and rider; one can't have it both ways, one must cut one's cloth according to one's purse, beggars can't be choosers. Mind you, I don't mind being reminded that this is unfortunately the kind of world in which we are living. But I have always resented the smug assumption that this is a reasonable state of affairs, and that on the whole it would be a worse world if one could have everything, if beggars could be choosers, if one could have the best of both worlds. There seems to be an hypocrisy, a fake humility, in pretending that one is bowing to reasonableness in accepting the limitations of human nature and the constrictive order of things as they are. What is so wonderful about the limitations of life that one should call it wisdom to idolize and idealize those limitations? The impossible is the only thing that's good enough for me."

"But that," I said, "is pure romanticism; that, if I may mix my metaphors, is like going into the garden and eating worms because one can't reach the moon."

"And what," my friend replied, "is wrong about romanticism? Rocket ships are, I am told, going to reach the moon, and voyages to the moon have long been imagined, as I recently learned in a book of that title. I intend to crave the impossible, to want everything; beggar though I am, to choose; to have, or to want the best of youth and age. There's no harm wishing. And what's more, the world designed according to my wishes would be, I think I could prove, a great deal more rational than the vulgar one that has only the banal distinction of existing. What's wrong with having everything, and at once? The earth isn't Heaven, but Heaven is still a better place than the earth, and it's from Paradise that I derive my standards. Do you have a better source?"

Every Century or So

Recently the papers published the obituary of the late Dean Hervey of the Columbia Law School, and mentioned as one of his recent activities a speech he gave to the South Carolina Society which, at its organization a hundred years ago, decided that it would listen to only one speech every century. That must have been an heretical decision to make in the most flourishing days of Southern oratory. The founder of that aristocratic coterie knew well enough how routine eloquence can become when listened to every month, or even every year. One pities the college chaplain or the college president who must annually make a commencement address. There is a challenge to say something non-fatuous, non-routine, to make of a stated occasion something striking and un-annual—a challenge infrequently met.

But to be told this is the first speech that has been made to this organization in one hundred years! There is a monition that must be paralyzing. It is almost as impossible to imagine as it would be impossible to live up to. The principle might be applied to writers. One ought to feel compelled always to say something world-shaking and stupendous, or to say nothing. To be put in the position of being the first voice to speak in a century! Out of the long silence one must come up with something worth saying. If a society waits a hundred years, one must give it something worth waiting for. One must do more than plagiarize what uncountable speakers have said for that hundred years. It is as if the whole world has been silent, waiting for the silence to break. What shall one say?

In the last century much has happened. We are at a crossing of the ways. What will the next hundred years bring us? It must be a brave man who would break the silence that has endured so long. Perhaps the bravest of all would be he who would wait for another hundred years, when at least some of the current confusion will presumably be cleared up. If it is not, then there will really be a silence; there will be no humanity at all waiting for the releasing word, the clarion call, the speech of the century—for there will not be any to listen or to talk. But if the world should continue to exist, the new issues that will have arisen will be no harder to resolve than those we have now. Certainly if one were asked, "Will you speak now or perhaps wait a century?" I think it might be well to wait a century for a better time to speak in, and undreamed-of points to speak on.

Da Capo

There are, as every day's headlines remind us, signs aplenty that we, the world, may be experiencing only another truce, longer or shorter, between a Second and Third World War. But there are signs too, perhaps subtly misleading, that we are in a fairly placid state, or at any rate that we think we are. The English Channel swimmers, I note, were busy again last summer. Only in a world where there was extra energy to spend would so many young people and some older ones be encouraged to indulge in such a wanton burst of energy. In an age where four-engined planes have become almost routine, fliers risk their lives, and some have already lost them, essaying to cross the Atlantic in a single-engined plane. Somebody has crossed the United States on a bicycle. New and complicated card games have become epidemic. College boys again are engaged in eating contests, which would have been unthought-of under rationing conditions. Pastel shades have returned to men's shirts. The blandishments of courtesy and flattery have returned to salesmen in the shops and even in the auto salons. And, in a grim way, the most encouraging thing of all, perhaps—a disaster to an excursion steamer (a mere handful of lives lost, by wartime standards) has shocked the imagination of the world almost more than the unimaginably larger casualties of a big battle. We have time now to be silly, to be extravagant, to be shocked, to be lavish with energy and emotion—as in the stringency of war, or imminent war, we have not.

All this, of course, would be encouraging, except that, to those of a certain age, there is a strange feeling of *da capo* about all this. Was it not in the 'twenties that there were competitions as to how long one could sit atop a flagpole? And was it not just before the depression that dance marathons were the vogue, and mah-jongg, and miniature golf? And are there not signs of just these things and their equivalents coming back? Was it not in the 'twenties that there were weekly flights by solo fliers, or duos, or trios, across the Atlantic and Pacific? Meanwhile, the tides of international tensions and economic crisis continue, now, as they did then. The vogue of the unimportant, the concern over the isolated disaster, are really not guarantees that the world is in order again. This normality has a familiar and suspicious ring.

(1949)

S-L-O-W

I am informed by reliable authority that a magazine entitled *Quick*, the most intransigently "digested" of the news weeklies, is a popular and financial success. Logically, it should be. If brevity is the essence of the matter, the briefer the better; and a magazine that can sum up the history of the week in ten minutes' reading time is patently better than one that takes twenty. The triumph of genius in this direction would of course be a publication that lucidly summarized the miscellaneous story of the past week of the world in one succinct and transparent sentence, or perhaps in one compact and not too cryptic word—an epithet, perhaps, that could be flashed in huge electric lights on the tower of some skyscraper. "There you have it!" one might say as he saw the comprehensive syllables flashed against the evening sky. Why bother about details? In essence, "This is it."

The trend all seems in this direction, but trends are notoriously reversible, and fashions generate their diametrical opposites. I suspect that in a few years there may be a mass market for a magazine called S-L-O-W. Such a publication would not necessarily be enormous in size, but there would be every internal indication that it was to be read slowly and, in the Baconian phrase, to be read, marked, and inwardly digested. For it is not only the news weeklies that have come to put a premium on speed of reading and the rapidity which which information may be acquired. The very style in which novelists write, or perhaps the lack of style with which they write, suggests that in fiction, too, we are being enjoined not to pause, not to savor, not to meditate nor reflect, but to skim along as rapidly as possible over the greatest miscellany of adventures, amorous and martial, that can be crowded into a thousand rapidly written, rapidly merchandised pages.

What a relief it would be to have a periodical which from its first page made it evident that what was here printed ought to be read slowly, to be thought about, to be savored, to be quietly enjoyed. Some of the popular magazines a few years ago used to put at the head of their stories: "Reading time: 11 minutes." It would be delightful to come across stories, poems, essays, for which, if the reading time were marked, it might conceivably be "the rest of your life," "eternity," "forever." Then there might be a revival of the art of literature, as against the purveying of information. The pleasures of the epicure would be renewed, and we should learn to taste rather than to gulp. The essay would replace the article; the novel would be more like a poem than like a piece of reportage; we should know fewer possibly irrelevant things less rapidly; we should apprehend them but slowly, slowly. We should come once again to perceive, to feel, to understand. But I suspect this transformation will itself be slow and that the dream publication called *S-L-O-W* is a long way off. Utopia time: a millennium.

What's He Like?

The other day a friend of mine mentioned with admiration the professional work of someone he did not realize I had long known.

"Oh, do you know him?" said my friend. "What's he like?"

I felt suddenly helplessly baffled. It is easy enough, coming home from a dinner or party where one has met a new acquaintance, possibly a celebrity, to explain glibly to one's friends what he is like. I summed up Nehru in a paragraph after meeting him at a crush tea. But it becomes increasingly difficult to be so glib the longer one knows a friend. The man in question I had known for something like twenty years. If anyone had said to me, "Do you know what he is like?" I should promptly have said, "Of course." But now, asked casually and without warning to tell what he was like, I found myself completely inarticulate.

How could I explain to someone who had never known the man what was most important or characteristic about him, and did I, I suddenly said to myself, really know? Perversely, there came into my mind at the moment all sorts of trivial, incidental, and superficial things. I thought of his somewhat affected manner, or what to a stranger would seem affected. I thought of little eccentricities of speech and of gesture—a preciousness of phrase, a prissiness of voice, a pompous stance. And it was on the tip of my tongue to say these things. But I had known this man too long to believe that these were his essence or his substance. I had seen him in moments of jubilation and despair. I knew his compassions and his intensities; I knew his affirmations and his doubts; I knew his little momentary malices and his deep moral indignation. It was impossible to make all these things clear in a moment or in an hour, and we did not have an hour.

"Oh, he's very nice," I said. "You would like him. We must arrange for you to meet him sometime."

"But you haven't told me what he's like," said my friend.

"I'm not sure I know," I said.

Know What I Mean?

It has become a familiar locution in colloquial New York speech, especially among the not very literate, after the most obvious sentence, to add "Y' know what I mean?" with a wistful, rising inflection implying that between "buddies," in the common brotherhood of men, among those who know their way around, explanations are unnecessary—and impossible. Thus, I have heard a taxi driver say, "I was just walking down the street; you know what I mean? I was going home and was going to stop for something to eat; you know what I mean?"

The expression has haunted me. There is something pathetic about it, and I wonder in what the pathos consists. Is it perhaps a shrewd suspicion on the part of those not accustomed to elaborate speech that even the simplest experience can somehow not be communicated, and that even walking down the street or stopping for something to eat is not quite explicable or communicable in its fullness? There is something about language, it is felt by those not professionally concerned with the arts of language, something that language cannot say. One might as well not try to say it, but just trust to luck, to a natural unspoken communion, to a sense that each solitary human being has, that *any* human being, any stranger, has been in the same boat, has been there, knows what it is like, will know what one means.

I have wondered why it has become so common to add the expression to the simplest utterances. Perhaps the New York equivalent of the London cockney who has never heard the name of Immanuel Kant is trying to say something like what Kant says in the *Critique of Judgment:* that, in life as in art, there is a felt meaning— and it is impossible to say what is meant; a realized purpose without the possibility of defining the purpose; a finality without the possibility of translating that finality into explicit speech. Perhaps the simple literate feels as Bergson felt, that all intellectual language is periphrastic, only the vaguest approximation. And yet that there is a communication, a viability, a communion beyond or below language. Know what I mean?

186

Cyclic Sense

Some of my middle-aged contemporaries are increasingly complaining that as the years go by they seem to go by more rapidly. And particularly to people in academic life there have come to be almost indecent rapidity and recurrence in the academic seasons. The shambles of registration are scarcely over when the whirlwind of examinations begins. One seems scarcely to have begun a course when one is giving his last lecture in it. The vacation season has hardly ended when the problem of what to do next summer begins.

All this is familiar enough, and so perhaps is the increasing sense of a rapidity in the cycle. Not only does time seem to move more rapidly, but it seems to return with whirlwind speed upon itself. I cannot help thinking that grandiose theories of returning cycles and recurrent ages are simply a projection of the human experience of repetition—repetition which, becoming more familiar as life goes on, seems to be more and more rapid in recurrence. By the time one is middle-aged, the wheels spin so rapidly that there is danger the cycle will settle down to a paradoxically fevered monotony. Everything seems to be the already seen, the previously experienced, the familiar round, and the recurrences begin to crowd one another until all is the vanity and sameness celebrated by Ecclesiastes.

Perhaps this explains why in life, as well as in novels, middle-aged persons suddenly, and to their friends' surprise, break out into unexpected nonconformities, violences, or madness. The reputable banker robs his bank; the happy, respectable householder deserts his household; there have even been cases of professors becoming ranchmen or movie extras or Bohemians or beachcombers.

How hard we are to please. We chafe at monotonies and recurrences, and almost in the same breath we complain about the insecurities and precariousness of the contemporary world, and look back to the pleasant life of security and of order we fondly believe to have been a delight of our Victorian ancestors. Perhaps these contradictory ideals of change and recurrence are not so contradictory as they seem. The very substance of life, the very fact of breathing, is itself a rhythm, and a rhythm is simply order among interruptions. Within the cycle of recurrence, there is plenty of variety possible. Though the weight of moral tradition is against it, it is possible in the cycle of change to enjoy both the expected and the surprising, to be alternately rested and thrilled.

Who? Me?

It is encouraging these days to hear so much said in defense of the individual. Only a few years ago the individual had threatened to be dissolved in a network of social relationships, and it was only by an illusion that one thought of oneself as a separate, unextinguishable, isolated, and inviolable being. The ego was no longer its own, but the function of a pattern of culture, of a tangle of complexes, the focus of a tradition, an organism, and an environment. Personality was an end-product of a social system. One was not oneself; one was the stereotype of a class, a family, a past, an infantile pattern, a racial memory.

It is almost worth a cold war to have a revival of rhetoric (anyway) about the dignity of the individual, the freedom of the unique personality, the inviolableness of the private being and the induplicable person. It is warming to the heart to sit back while democratic orators remind one how precious and ultimate one is. It is the individual for whom wars of liberation are fought, the liberty of the individual for which heroes die, the private soul for whom the elaborate machinery of democratic life is justified. The least of us is as much as the greatest. Nobody can be more than one, and any one of us illustrates all the dignity, freedom, and preciousness of the most beautiful and flowering genius among us.

When orators begin to talk of the ultimate dignity of the individual, I like to think they might just as well be meaning me. Surely it is inspiring to think that any of us is as mighty an illustration of justice and worth as the most eminent or the most useful or the most generous. The individual, Lord bless him! The individual, more power to him! The individual, the summit of human endeavor! The Individual! Heavens, he *is* talking about me!

The Autobiography of a Symptom

Descartes, sitting by his Dutch stove, could reduce to a minimum the furniture of his assumptions. He could have the psychological security of thinking that, at least so long as he thought, he existed. Schopenhauer could argue that so long as he was aware of desire, he could be jolly well (though "jolly" hardly seems the word for Schopenhauer) certain that he was really real. And there are various other fashions of retreating to the impregnable height of soliloquy and private awareness.

In an age given over to regimentation by external things, and regimentation by governmental agencies, one welcomes all movements in thought, in art, and in action, which reaffirm the quality of individual life, of irreducible personality. One applauds even small instances of the little flame of selfhood asserting itself against the dampening forces of the big, the grandiose, and the general. That is why we turn so avidly, I think, to the biographies or autobiographies of the mavericks and exceptions in our time. Something speaks to our own wistful and constricted hearts when a Gauguin goes off to the South Seas; when a well-established advertising agent becomes a mystic monk; when, in one way or another, an individual tries to make his life bear unmistakably his own signature, bespeak his own vanities.

And in our personal lives, when we find signs in ourselves that we are speaking in our own accent, speaking our own minds, living by our own opinions, we feel the pulse-beat of our own personality coming to life again. We feel that in having discovered or arrived at ourselves, we have discovered a continent which is all our own.

This gratifying discovery or achievement of the self is always threatened, however, and poisoned by the contemporary passion for statistics. It turns out, alas, that the autobiography of each of us is a symptom. The nuances even of our revolts and our originalities turn out to be instances of a statistical tendency. After all, one discovers, one is not the only one who flees regimentation. There is a whole regiment of rebels, all rebelling at the same place and in the same way. It is discouraging to think that one is not alone in wishing to be one's self. Privately and patiently, one has reflected on the inadequacies of national sovereignty, only to find oneself in a whole battalion of those who long for world federation. If one feels he is beyond all conventional groups and a unique devotee of nihilism and chaos, it is humiliating to find thousands of existentialists who are saying and feeling exactly the same thing.

On a bus I heard a young girl describing, to her friend, a young man whom she clearly admired. "He is," she said, "an original-type young man." That is the last infirmity and humiliation. One struggles to be independent, to be unique, to be one's self, only to find one illustrates a statistical tendency, helps define the curved lines on a chart. One guards the flame of one's own personality only to find this flame is a quite familiar type of flame; at best, one has fallen into the stereotype of genius, into the mildly superior rut of originality. Autobiography is becoming so popular an art that a writer can scarcely wait until he is twenty-five before publishing a story of his life. Someday soon, I expect to see such a personal record with a statistically honest title: *The Autobiography of a Symptom.*

Alibi for Dullness

I am told, though not on very good authority (the friend of a friend of a second vice-president), that a certain large corporation requires executives above a certain grade to have an indeterminate number of hours of casualness every day. These periods of silence are naturally not to be at stated times; they are to be as random as life itself. Apparently the president of the corporation had been reading some efficiency magazine, published, unknown to himself, by a subsidiary of his corporation. In an article written by a professor of business administration, it was reported that the head of a billion-dollar industrial organization had found he got his best ideas when he was doing absolutely nothing; that the busier he was, the less creative thought he produced. Of late, since he had been promoted to chairman of the board and had had nothing whatever to do, he had been so filled with ideas that the new president of the corporation was busier than ever putting them into operation. The corporation had never declared such high profits as since its chairman of the board had had nothing to do but to think casually.

It has certainly occurred to many of us in moments of extreme busyness that if only we had time to think we should be fountainheads of creative ideas. In the noise of busy days, we light upon notions that we are too busy later to remember, too pressed immediately to develop. It occurs to us that if only we were really free, how many fertile hypotheses we should engender, how our unfrustrated genius would flower! We think of Poincaré, the mathematician, walking along the seashore and having his most crucial ideas come to focus in contemplating the pebbles on the beach. We think of Newton under the apple tree, of Housman walking nonchalantly along a country road after lunch.

It is a little humiliating to be granted suddenly the blessed gift of leisure. One listens for the murmur of the Subconscious; one cups one's ear for the whisper of the liberating disclosure. Nothing happens; all is vast emptiness, a desert of dullness. It is perhaps summer in a remote place with no interruptions. There is for us not a single commitment, social or professional. Now, if ever, is the time when the creative wave should begin, the creative seed grow and blossom. Nothing occurs.

Perhaps, then, one says to one's self, what one really needs is the friction and stimulation of other minds, the crush of action out of which ideas have always emerged. Perhaps what is lacking is the catalysis of work, the urgency of a deadline. Perhaps what is wrong, comes the blushing realization, is one's self.

The Inside Story

It is both discouraging and amusing to read the accounts published in the newspapers of some event about the details of which one happens to be informed at first hand. Even in the most scrupulous report there is something wrong or something missing. Especially is one tempted to smile at interpretations by reporters or commentators, and most especially when explanations are given of motives or of character. One always knows so much better. There are facts not in the public record; there are details knowable only through long intimacy with one of the persons involved.

It is, of course, easy to generalize, and there is a natural assumption that what is true in instances one does know about is equally true about affairs to which one is a stranger. It is impossible to read of public events these days without wondering what the private facts are. There are curtains—silk, iron, ironic—by which, one is certain, the inner realities of our age are concealed. There are many Kremlins outside Russia, whose secrets, too, are guarded. All this explains the vogue of the gossip column, the personal interview, the growing literature of exposé and confession. Here, one thinks, is the low-down, the real McCoy, the disclosure that lights up everything, the payoff, the revelation. We are beginning to live again in an age of whispers. The wildest rumor, if attributed to some confidential source, an ex-friend or ex-butler, has more authority than a bureau of economic research, or a council of foreign relations.

We are living, as Bertrand Russell once suggested, in an alien world. Even in our own country we feel that we are outsiders. But trust us to try to get the inside story about war and peace from friends of friends of prime ministers, about the universe itself from eavesdroppers of confidants of ministers of God.

The Ambiguities

My friend Flicker is always in a state of perfectly divided soul. He is so fair to all sides that he cannot come to any conclusion. He is particularly troubled now by the arguments pro and con concerning the unintelligibility of modern poetry, and, for that matter, a good deal of modern prose. "I'm simply at an impasse," he said to me the other day as he came in loaded down with half a dozen books of the new criticism and the old. "I used to feel free to condemn a poem for being unintelligible, but not now. I have been taught better. I know that language is, in the hands of the creative, an experiment. The clearly intelligible is the cliché. The true artist explores the remote mountainlands of language, its high passes, its dangerous ravines. He scorns words with but a single level of meaning; or, to change the metaphor, he despises the counters of common human interchange."

"A very good case for the difficult in poetry," I observed. "Why do you have any uneasiness at all?"

He wiped his brow. "Oh, but I've been reading some of the older critics," he said, "and I find that a classic writer is one who speaks with the simplest directness about simple ultimate things. Homer keeps his eye, Matthew Arnold says, on the object. He shows us the thing in itself as it really is. He speaks in the great centralities of human feeling. The obscure is likely to be the eccentric, the subtle the parochial, the affectedly private the occupation of an always doomed coterie. The true classic is humanity itself on the level of genius, an exquisitely articulated cry of the general human heart. It spans the parochialisms of class and time and education. It is the secular religion, the creative communion of all mankind. It is everyman speaking to everyman. And is not poetry, as a great romantic once said, simple, sensuous, and passionate? What do the new critics have to say to that? You can understand that I am a little bewildered."

"What do you propose to do?" I said.

"I don't know," he said, greatly troubled. "Shall I give up classic poetry or modern poetry, or the critics?"

"Give up the critics," I said.

"That's rather what I had been thinking." And, sorting out his books, he said, "I shall leave the rest with you." He left with one volume of Milton and one of Dylan Thomas under his arm.

Nothing

A novel has recently appeared, quite a superior one, too, entitled *Nothing*. It is not uncommon to have had works of fiction entitled with one omnivorous word: *Steel, Brass, Bread, Loving, Persuasion, Victory*. The word is usually a clue to the theme or to some recognizable range of human experience. But a book entitled *Nothing* is a challenge. Henry Green, the author of the novel, describes it as "a frivolous comedy of manners." The book ends with the middle-aged "hero" saying to the middle-aged "heroine" (in reply to her question, "And is there nothing else at all you want, my own?"), "Nothing—nothing," as he falls asleep.

But the mind strays from the actual story so entitled to other books that might well have been called by the same name. Bergson, it will be remembered, devotes some fascinating pages to the idea of Nothing and the difficulty in imagining it. Mystic theologians, desperately attempting to define God, have, like Dionysius the Areopagite, ended in a negative theology. God, the mystics have frequently insisted, must be nameless because to name him specifically is to limit his being, and the line between the One and the None is very hard to draw. One of the reasons that even the most gifted poets have had trouble reporting ecstasy is that, in so exalted a state, distinctions are transcended and all becomes "one luminously transparent conscious moment." But consciousness of what—everything? Perhaps it would be better to say "nothing."

One's imagination plays over some possible contemporary uses for this peculiar title. Could not some of our futilitarian interpreters of history, writing on the prospects of mankind, sum up their researches and conclusions with this most negative of words? Could not the word "nothing" be used over and over again by novelists if they were accurately to identify the significance of the characters and the action in their stories? Could not all the inconclusive and ambiguous reflections on the present time be interpreted as sound and fury signifying, as every high school student knows, *nothing*?

Let Us Now Praise . . .

It is a cliché to say that it is easier—and more amusing—to damn than to praise. This familiar reflection never comes so acutely to awareness as when one is attending a testimonial dinner to some distinguished person on the occasion of anything from his fiftieth to his ninetieth birthday. The reflection becomes sharp to the point of pain if one is a scheduled speaker, and rather late in the schedule. By the time one rises to speak, virtually every laudable aspect of the guest of honor has been broached, developed, embroidered, extrapolated—until anything more seems less a labor of love than a work of redundance.

Granted that the man is the demi-paragon who has prompted the dinner in the first place. Agreed that there never was such a teacher, so communicative, so radiant, at once so flexible and so conscientious, so imaginative and responsible, so creative and faithful. He is, it goes without saying—except that it has been said about a dozen times already—marked by the most perceptive seriousness and the most bubbling humor. Age has not withered him, however much by this time in the evening the speakers have withered the audience.

Despite the fact that one has come as an act of piety, how almost irresistible is the temptation to arise and speak, not the forthright truth, but the most violent and malicious lies. The guest of honor himself, and certainly the audience, would be enormously relieved suddenly to hear that this paragon of academic animals was really a rake and a vulture, a double-dealer and a scoundrel, that, as was said at Oxford about the classicist, Jebb, "What time he could spare from the adornment of his person he devoted to the neglect of his duties."

The more scabrous one's accusations, the more relaxed the guest of honor would become, for, undoubtedly, in his sweet and patient life he has long cherished the private dream of being a secret villain, and the fantasy of having long and deliberately deceived his ardent and faithful public. How the audience would revive, too, for by this time in the evening the principle of Aristides the Just, has begun to operate, and everyone feels that no one could possibly be *that* good. And have we not been taught in our generation, beginning with the debunking 'twenties, that the adjective natural to truth is "unpleasant," and that revelations are never of divinity, but of clay feet?

There is a very good reason why, on such an occasion of pious tribute, one does not quite dare to blurt out the unspeakable, mention the unmentionable, and report the seamy side of the guest of honor. For if one did, it is more than likely that the audience would be saying to itself, "How whimsical really! He couldn't possibly mean it, but isn't it fun to hear him say these dreadful things in fun?" The mood of piety has become so mellow that anything unpleasant, if it happens to be uttered, is regarded as the sheerest fantasy of pious good humor.

"Well," the last speaker says to himself before he rises, "I may as well keep to the temper of the evening." He begins, inevitably, "Everything that ought to be said about our guest of honor has already been said, but I shall take just a few moments of your time to add a few words." The moments lengthen into minutes, the minutes seem to be hours. Somewhere along toward midnight the toastmaster, who is famous for his gift of words, says, "Our revels now are ended." But only after the guest of honor has arisen to say in a succinct forty minutes that he deserves none of the praises that have been lavished on him, and that he realizes that the tribute is not to him, but to education, to religion, to democracy, to humanity, to the past, to the future, to our cultural inheritance, and to posterity—all of which, in his poor way, he has tried to serve.

The Prospect Before Us

An English friend wrote me early last summer regretting that I had been compelled to postpone for a year a visit to England. His regret was tempered by cheerfulness and a certain real relief about my presumable mental health. "It *did* seem to me," he wrote, "quite a lunatic thing for you to propose to yourself to come over here while the Labour government is still in power. By next year they will be gone and you will recognize English civilization again."

At this writing I do not know how good a prophet my friend is; I do know he has been hopefully predicting the end of the Labour government for about five years now. Nor am I citing his political judgment with approval. What does interest me about his explosion is the comforting sense he has that a change in administration will make everything fine again. That is, he wishes to be back in the Edwardian—better still, the Victorian—era. In his mind's eye, I have no doubt, he sees hansom cabs once more rolling on the recobbled streets of London, and the great houses in Portland Square each smoothly served by a staff of housemaids and footmen superintended by an impeccable butler.

My friend knows better, of course, but, like many people in late middle age, he has an irresistible hope that the clock will be turned back, and he believes that all that is required is the reinstatement of a backward-looking political party to achieve such a miraculous chronological reversion. There is a whole age group, those between fifty and sixty, to whom Utopia is not in the far future or in the inconceivably distant past. The date of the end of paradise is 1914. The calendar there marks the close, in this country as well as in England, of an epoch that, seen through the eyes of nostalgia, looks miraculously simple and serene. It was an age in which international peace was not a problem but a fact. It was a period without the frustration of traffic lights. It was a time when one could use the word "progress" seriously, and believe that the path of progress was indefinitely open before us.

"Throw the rascals out" is a familiar political sentiment; and, by the most impeccable logic, the rascals to be thrown out are the very ones who at the moment happen to be in. But the scoundrels now to be ejected are more than political opponents. They have become moral symbols. It is really devils whom the nostalgic wish to throw out, the big devils of present actuality, the more distant devils of future monstrosity. No wonder my English friend wrote me to come next year, when things will be more or less as they had been before. Bicycles will glide quietly over motorless streets; the click of mallet against croquet ball will be heard on the beautifully kept lawns of country houses; there will be vast feasts and plans for passport-less imperial travel. Perhaps at a dinner party someone may suggest that things look a little uneasy in the Balkans, or someone else, like Max Beerbohm's immortal T. Fenning Dodsworth, will say he does not like the look of things in the Far East. But both gentlemen will be set down as eccentric alarmists; the port and the nuts will be passed round; all will be wonderfully at peace.

My friend would indignantly deny that he really believes all this, but in his kind old Tory heart I am certain he half does.

Sic Transit

A macabre practical joker once appeared at the front door in the middle of a dinner party given by an older friend of mine, then a very lively dean. The man insisted on seeing the head of the house; and when the host appeared at the door, the visitor turned out to represent a local undertaking firm. He had come on a telephoned request to take charge of the body of our host, who was intelligibly not amused.

At a large university recently, an eminent scholar, who had reason to believe his writings were fairly well known, had a similar experience. The Secretary turned over to him a letter addressed to the University from a small town in California. The letter inquired whether the University would enable the correspondent to "contact" the scholar in question. "He was," so the letter ran, "connected with your university, I believe, about twenty-five years ago. If you would give me his present whereabouts, I should greatly appreciate it. I have no way of knowing what has become of him." The eminent thinker brooded over this missive.

Everyone broods at some time or another over the obscurity, the anonymity, the zero place of his own personality in his era. Swift is said to have remarked when he looked, years after its writing, at *A Tale of a Tub:* "My God, I had genius when I wrote that." Many another writer, looking at an early work of his own, can only reflect on how long forgotten it is. Max Beerbohm once found in a secondhand bookshop a book that long ago he had "affectionately" inscribed to a friend. He bought the book, wrote in it "still affectionately," and mailed it to the friend who had disposed of it.

How often one meets the ghosts of former celebrities, men and women whose names once meant something to practically every literate person. It is a shock that they are still alive; one feels it would have been much more decent and proper of them to have been buried with their reputations. They have no right to be perambulating in so belated a living air. They constitute reminders, too discouraging, of the transiency of fame.

My friend replied to the inquiry as to what had become of him that he presumed he was still identical with the person being sought. But was he? Are we not all distant echoes of earlier selves, of transformed personalities going by the same name? "Whatever has become of so and so?" we ask. Whatever has become of me, one sometimes asks himself or should ask. But—the consoling thought comes to us—our essential being, our authentic self, has changed no more than (until very old age) our own familiar voice changes. It is only the public mask of one stage of our lives that has vanished. Thus, the modishness of a given art critic may have disappeared, but his delight in art itself may last freshly and happily through his obscure last years. Marcus Aurelius warned us against relying upon the externalities of wealth, of friends, of fame. He followed his own warning and retired into the fortress of his own soliloquy. It is not his fault that by so doing he insured his future fame. While he was still alive, there must have been someone in some remote corner of the Roman Empire who asked, "What *has* become of Marcus Aurelius?"—or, when he passed by in some place remote from Rome, "Now *who* on earth is that?"

Syntopicon

The Encyclopaedia Britannica, in cooperation with the University of Chicago, is issuing, or may by this time have issued, a two-volume dictionary of the three thousand ideas which are allegedly the subjects of discussion in the Great Books. The topics include such matters as Truth, Wisdom, Justice, Good and Evil (these two, possibly, we are told, mergeable into one). All the great authors from Plato to (at random) Goethe, are carrying on a conversation, always unbeknownst to one another, answering one another. For it is clear that Plato could not have *known* he was answering David Hume or John Stuart Mill.

The Great Writers, it seems, had the Great Ideas, and the Great Themes number about three thousand. They are all neatly codified in what is called a *Syntopicon*. One would like to undertake a similar dictionary of the Not So Great Ideas, the Modest Themes that have been the subject-matter of less ambitious conversations from Primitive Man to, say, Thomas Mann—the latter in his more relaxed moments with family friends. One is willing to wager that the Weather would have a good many entries in such an index. Spring—Late, Early, Cold, Wet; Summer—Dry, Rainy. . . . The High Cost of Living would doubtless also have a good many references, even in the eighteenth century, even in salons where grand ladies discussed philosophy. Marriages Hinted At, Divorces Imminent, Romances Rumored—I suspect all these would be no small part of the *Syntopicon* of Ideas which have really strayed into the conversation of even so urbane a society as would or could spend five hundred dollars on a set of books, the cost of the first edition of the Chicago Great Books. And as for those eternal questions which enter into the Great Conversation: What Did He See in Her, or She in Him? There is no doubt that they would have to go into our, admittedly, minor *Syntopicon*, too.

The War, with Inflections

The commentators lost their following in the years of uneasy peace; they are regaining it now that war and rumors of greater wars are back with us. In a large city one is not dependent on radio. But cut off during the summer from daily newspapers, on a remote ranch in Wyoming, I found myself listening to them again. The best were as good as ever, the worst even worse. And, with radio reception erratic in a mountain area, one settled for what one could get, when one could get it.

Radio commentators provide an excellent lesson showing how much of language depends on inflection, how delicate is the line between fact and opinion. How quickly one learns to trust the dry, succinct Indiana speech of Elmer Davis; how promptly to note the quiet distinction he makes between his opinion and the facts he is reporting, sometimes by the faintest modulation, or by the parenthesis of half a sentence. How quickly revolted one becomes by those who use a war and men dying in it for their own political hobbies of hate or for their own bland patrioteering—verbal warriors safe in the quiet and security of a radio studio.

Doubtless television reveals even more by the expression of the face of the commentator. Insincerity is even harder to conceal from the eye than from the ear. But the voice alone is enough. Smugness comes unmistakably over the air waves, and how rapidly, too, one senses the cheapness of personalities who with whipped-up cheerfulness or melodrama serve each day's grist of anxiety and horror. It is, doubtless, possible to be as vulgar in print as by word of mouth, as exhibitionistic and as insincere. Some of the leading political columnists seem to prove this. But the blandness, the smugness, the transparent homefront heroics, the mouthing into condescending clichés of even the deepest principles of democratic faith, all these sound worse by voice than they look on the printed page. A sneer at our enemies, self-congratulation—all this brings out the worst in the way of war neuroses. There is spiritual as well as material profiteering that goes on in wartime. It is a comfort to find, once in a way, the intonations of integrity, of modesty, of responsibility, of truth. One recognizes these virtues in an inflection; one knows them almost without the words. Sometimes a voice speaks that sounds as if it were truth itself that were doing the talking—truth, quiet and clear, speaking with authority.

The Fairly Good Listener

Occasionally one hears it said of someone or other that he's a very good listener, occasionally even that she is. The picture springs to one's mind of a rapt figure, all radiant attention, listening (perhaps to oneself) as if a revelation from Heaven were being given. Long experience of talking and listening affords, perhaps, a different view of the matter.

The art of good listening is, one suspects, a highly histrionic business. The important thing in acquiring a reputation for having so cherished a social asset is to look the part. It is possible to achieve the mask of flatteringly intent concentration on what someone else is saying. The mind is, of course, free to wander elsewhere. All that is needed is the little trick of murmuring occasionally a "Yes, indeed!" . . . "But no!" or even that dreary expression used by chronological or permanent teen-agers, "You are so right." There is a legend that a famous mathematician, widely known as a good listener, worked out a knotty point in the theory of functions while politely listening to a lady give an account of her travels in Portugal. There are certain social virtuosi who manage, while they are talking themselves, to hear what is being said all over the room. One famous male gossip remained a mystery to his friends. One could scarcely get a word in edgewise when one met him. But clearly he must sometimes have listened, for he was full of knowledge by hearsay of rumors that had never yet been seen in print.

Some people, with the best will in the world, cannot be good listeners, for they are highly allergic to bores. They really *do* listen hard for as long as they are able—which is a very brief period. Sometimes if the bore one is listening to is a resounding bore, one is driven to start, and to keep, talking, not because one wants to say anything, or because one has the slightest interest in what one is saying. One talks in a private filibuster only in self-defense, only not to hear that fearful voice begin again, only not to listen again to tales of boring controversy, of outlandish theory, of cliché philosophy, of big-game-shooting in Kenya, of hands once held in bridge, of scores made in golf, of meals eaten in Venice, of glib analyses of Korea and Formosa and Greece. At times the bore whom one has by sheer momentum quenched seems in his (or her) turn to be listening with passionate absorption. Or is it with glazed eyes? A new attack is doubtless being planned, one well knows, behind that mask of polite attention. Soon the barrage of soliloquy will begin again. Just keep talking, one says to oneself. This is, of course, no way to get a reputation for being a good listener. But the chances are even that in this quite accidental fashion one may get to be known as a wonderful conversationalist.

One Can't Go There Again

There is a melancholy pleasure in returning to the same place at least two summers in succession, especially a place in which one last year had become part of a small and agreeable community. There is always a touch of sadness about such a return, the shadow that at once darkens and deepens one's enjoyment. One looks for the same *time*-marks and they are still there, not only a stable landmark like a towering mountain, or cliff, or cape, but the light at just this angle on an August afternoon, with its fading gold tinctured with thoughts of autumn and the dying year and of years done and to come. One notes, on the other hand, conspicuous absence; people have died, and some have simply stayed away. And one misses the person one was oneself last year, and the world one had known a year ago, so talkative about possible war, so unbelieving of it.

The children of some of one's friends have grown a year older, too. The twelve-year-old girl has become thirteen, and suddenly the young woman she is to be is imminent in her manners and her looks. The boy one had known only a year ago as a child has this year begun to talk of college, or the Army. The sense of mortality and change assails one, especially about the young. It is not only that the young in our time (even the girls) have as good a chance of dying as the old, and conveniently at home, too, in their own houses, on familiar streets. Something less world-wide and non-political enforces the sense

217

of transformation as an older person looks at his juniors. How many children has one seen change from children to adults! One ought to be accustomed to it by now, and one surely could not want children to stay childish forever. The thought, even, is a horrid blend of monstrosity and sentimentalism. One does not wish the caterpillar to stay a caterpillar, nor the possible frog a mere tadpole. One is sometimes, to speak bluntly, relieved to think forward to the time when the squalling child will be an adolescent, to the period when the adolescent will be a man. But these children one had known have died as surely as if they had perished. The adults one suddenly knows are different persons, possibly totally different. Oneself will be to these recently hatched adults a memory of childhood. There will, later, of course, be other children who will come into view, but they will be strangers, too; and they, in time, if one lives long enough to see them grow up, will be strangers once more—different ones.

Perhaps it is wiser to go to a new place, to see it only once, to have it remain a frozen instant of memory, to be a possession as long as one lives. Nothing need change a recollection not rechecked by experience; what is recalled can remain consonant with that now remote moment of happiness. It is, perhaps, lucky for the travel agencies that this is so. One must get away from here; one cannot go back there.

Not for an Age?

It was a little picnic on an August mountainside overlooking a valley in the Tetons. Somebody had thought to bring along a volume of poetry, quaintly Tennyson, and the small group were by happy chance in the mood to hear poetry read aloud. The reader, himself a poet, read some of the early works, "Oriana," "Lady Clara Vere de Vere," "Airy, Fairy Lillian." We smiled condescendingly. How we had outgrown all that! How quaint was Victorian feeling and Victorian fashion! And even in some of the better, indeed the best, of Tennyson, was there not pseudo-Grecian feeling corrupting the classic Greek flavor? Did not Lucretius sound as if he were in London in 1860, a member of the Metaphysical Society? Was there not a touch of Sir Richard Burton in "Ulysses"?

Later in the day, thinking back to the episode, I began to wonder how much of the feeling that now, when expressed, seems so timeless and so independent of our era is nonetheless, as it will be seen shortly, say in fifty years, to be, a quaintness, a period piece, an oddity. But one insists to oneself, "There is nothing chronologically provincial about me. I see around everything purely contemporary. I am a spectator, like Plato, of all time and all existence. Knowing about culture patterns, I have freed myself from them. Have I not learned, too, from Freud and the anthropologists not to take my prejudices or my society too absolutely? Have I not read the semanticists and freed myself from temporary connotations?

Could anyone be better equipped than we are to free ourselves from the conventions which bound earlier generations? Have we not seen around Marx and around liberalism and around Newton, even?"

Suddenly one hears the low voice of posterity: "How alike they all sound, the whole kit and caboodle of them in the 1950's, with their culture patterns, their complexes, their fright of the new atomic age. How sure they were that civilization was at an end; how filled they were with despair, of man and all his works, including atomic fission." The voice sinks to a faint whisper: "There were one or two original minds, but nobody paid any attention to them." The voice trailed off almost into silence. For the life of me I could not make out what the names were. The voice repeated them, but, since I had never heard them before, they meant nothing to me, and I forgot them at once. But I was somehow certain they were neither Russian nor American, and the voice almost inaudibly murmured the slogan of a philosophy which I had never heard mentioned, even by the *avant-garde*. It was shocking to be told, almost in so many words, that we are not for (or of) all time, but for an age only, our age —perhaps, as some believe, almost over.

Self-Help in the Midst of Doom

The publishers, it is clear, are making the best of two areas of pay dirt, one of doom and one of self-improvement. H. G. Wells once said that the future was a race between education and catastrophe. The publishing lists are crowded with predictions of evil things to come and helpful little volumes that promise to mature your mind, to bring peace to your soul, to lift up your heart, to civilize your manners, to relax your tensions, to ennoble your character, to force people to love you, to persuade you to love them.

It is confusing to find in the same page an advertisement of one book that proves that the end of civilization is unavoidable, and next to it the rapturous announcement of another book that will enable you in the brief interval before universal oblivion to salvage your soul and to retrieve your body, that will bring you wealth, health, happiness—all this before the obliteration of everything.

"In a whistling void I stand before my mirror / Unconcerned, and tie my tie," Conrad Aiken once wrote in a poem. Some of the prophets of doom make us feel that our situation is even more futile. We have fears not only that we may cease to be, but that the planet may cease to whirl. It is all the more surprising therefore that so many people should be concerned, even up to the extravagance of buying a book, with remodeling their characters, improving their minds, or finding peace for their psyches. It perhaps speaks well for the moral sense of the American people that in the midst of a world crisis whose resolution no one can foretell, publishers should find it profitable to republish a standard work on etiquette, or that a volume of streamlined psychoanalysis—dianetics—should be so widely read.

Could it possibly be true that people are taking the crisis less seriously than they suppose? Could it be that in our hearts we still believe there is an off-chance that the human race may survive and that there will still be a world? Are not all those who buy the self-help books acting on the principle of "just in case."—Just in *case* civilization *should* survive, it would be both agreeable and useful to have a quiet mind, a happy heart, good manners, maturity, friends, and influence.

Or are the self-help books really another form of escape literature? In a world of mounting tension, it is soothing for an hour or two to curl up with a book that, though it makes no promise to save civilization, says it can render you more mature, lovable, and delightful.

Universal solutions for the world's ills are more tentatively offered than they used to be. The world may be in a bad way, but there are still little books calculated to reassure the individual. When the crack of doom comes, it will strike down, in the readers of self-help primers, charming, poised, serene, and cultured victims. Meanwhile, while one writer tells us "it is later than you think," it is not too late to buy a book that will help you to "look younger and live longer"—provided it is possible to live at all.

Le Temps Gelé

Sometimes one has a succession of shocking moments when one has irrefutable evidence that one is middle-aged. A spectacular instance of that discovery is to come upon some recent textbook on American history, in particular to read its last three or four chapters. It turns out that students in college are now studying as history and as an epoch what was the living environment of one's own childhood and youth.

"What," one asks, "is going on here?" History, clearly, ended with the Civil War, or certainly not later than the Spanish-American War. When I was a child of five or six I remember someone in our house singing a song of "old, unhappy, far-off things, and battles long ago." And what were the unhappy, far-off things? Well, this is the way the song ran:

> Spain, Spain, Spain,
> You ought to be ashame'
> For doing such a thing
> As blowing up the Maine.

I was only two years old when the Maine was blown up, and it took me a few years to get around to the news, even in song. The Civil War, history? Yes. The Spanish-American War, history? Granted.

But it is extremely confusing, not to say discouraging, to realize that the First World War is now regarded as history, something to be written down in textbooks and debated by historians. Woodrow Wilson an historical figure? A small boy in Sea Girt, New Jersey, once shook hands with the then Governor Woodrow Wilson. No living person ever shook hands with Alexander the Great, Julius Caesar, or Napoleon. History ought to have the decency to wait until one is dead, and the days of one's youth ought not to become the palimpsests and papyri of one's juniors while one is still alive.

The historians are becoming indecently hasty. "Let the dead Past bury its dead" is all right, but there is no injunction for historians to bury the living memories of the middle-aged. In the constantly losing warfare of a teacher to make things sound timely and apposite, one mentions to a group of freshmen Pearl Harbor, D-Day, V-J Day, and they look as if old Nestor were telling them epic events of the incredibly remote past.

There are certain compensations, however. "And did you once see Shelley plain?" Not Shelley, my children, but Bernard Shaw, Woodrow Wilson, Bergson, Havelock Ellis, Edwin Arlington Robinson.

I once heard Nicholas Murray Butler, who had been reminiscing about eminent historical figures he had known (Bismarck for one), remark, "You can't get history out of the textbooks; you've got to know the people," or at least know those who knew them. There is some satisfaction in having one's own memories, perhaps, serve as a footnote, and to substitute for a sense of being alive a sense of having part of one's life already become, however minutely, a part of history.

Wars—and How to Live Through Them

I came across an essay the other day, or rather that hybrid literary genre known as an article, in which a veteran war correspondent was writing what was, in effect, a brief handbook for civilians in the next, and, as the article implied, inevitable war. There were a few simple rules which, though they might not stop the war, might make one feel better. One was that one should not be afraid, and another was that one should not be too distressed, and a third one was that one should not expect the worst. There were still other delightful suggestions— for example, "One should go on with one's normal activities." Mr. Leland Stowe, the author of this guidebook on how to behave in the midst of slaughter, tells us that some of the best parties he ever attended were given in Madrid while bombs were falling.

There was a series of rules issued by the State Department last summer on what to do if and when an atom bomb falls. There were about eight rules, six or seven of which one would undoubtedly not have time to collect one's thoughts about in the minute or so provided before annihilation. It is very reassuring, therefore, to be told by Mr. Stowe that it is all very simple. All that is necessary is to go on living precisely as if there weren't a war going on.

There are, clearly, little difficulties that he glosses over. There were a great many people during the last war who would have been quite content, for example, to go on smoking a pack of cigarettes a day, if they could have found them; quite content not to be afraid of anything (even when the earth under them trembled), especially not the end of civilization. Hegel is said to have gone on writing his elaborate abstractions, his "ballet of bloodless categories," while the Battle of Jena was going on virtually at his doorstep. At the end of three days he is said to have called somewhat irritably to his servant and asked, "What is all that noise going on?"

The ostrich used to be criticized for doing what he usually does, burying his head in the sand. But it is now clear that the ostrich, not the owl, is the true symbol of wisdom. The ostrich is going on with its standard procedure of burying its head in the sand. That makes all the rest easy. There is nothing to see and therefore nothing to fear; there is nothing to be distressed about. Presumably, with one's head buried in the sand, one would not even *hear* a battle. There are born city-dwellers who are wonderfully impervious to noise; well, given a few more years of crisis, one can learn to be impervious even to the sounds of doom. Apparently it needs a good first-class war to bring true peace of mind. In an age where gentleness has vanished, it is possible still to be a gentleman.

Scene Behind the Scene

A popular novel was published the other day (in the British use of "the other day," meaning anywhere from the other day to ten years ago) in which the author, a woman, in a preface, took the reader into her confidence. She explained the various places in which, the various circumstances under which, the various distractions and hardships through which, she had produced this marketable masterpiece. It was, as one reviewer remarked, as if a hostess should just before dinner recite all the troubles she had had preparing it. Other authors, Henry James (if it is not too disrespectful to mention that master in this connection) for one, have been like cooks sharing their recipes.

One looks back somewhat wistfully to the days when one could at least pick up a novel, without having a prefatory natural history, a foreword of explanation and apology, a note of exposition of what the author intended and what the author directs the reader to find. The trend in works other than fiction has been similar. We are not left to begin a treatise on culture patterns or isotopes without a narration of how the author happened to get interested in the subject—he was inspired, perhaps, by a great humane genius of a teacher who unfortunately for the world had developed writer's cramp in early youth and had therefore to confine the spread of his wisdom to those in his small classes in the remote college village in the Southern Appalachians where the author, by luck, had studied under him in a course in freshman English. Or perhaps the writer, a corporation lawyer, had come to spend all his leisure hours in the study of bees or the literature of bees, his initial impulse having come from the sting of a bee which, when the pain subsided, had prompted him to that "emotion recollected in tranquillity" which does not always become poetry, but sometimes pedantry. Or, again, the writer may be one of those indefatigable encyclopedists-on-the-run who every year or two write a book on the inside of a country, a continent, or a cosmos. The reader is invited first to peruse the immense travels and travails of the author; even the labors of his staff are sometimes mentioned. Finally, even a new dictionary may parade in advance not simply the quality but the quantity of contributors, and the apparatus of cross-indices and filing cards, which has gone into the preparation of this paragon of portmanteau knowledge.

Often in the glossy pages of the general magazines one finds advertisements of bottles of soft drinks embedded in flowers, or of Chippendale television sets which are clearly the preconditions of "gracious living." There was a time when "gracious living" had as one of its conditions the concealing from guests of the trouble and care that had gone into the provision of food and entertainment. It was considered the duty of the host not to mention family troubles or private distress. There was a time when one read a book for itself and not to share the labors and endurances of the author. "I wrote this sonnet in fifteen minutes," remarks Molière's Oronte. The reply made to him is, "Monsieur, time doesn't count in these matters."

"It took me four hard years of the most arduous research to write this book," we are assured by the writer of some *soi-disant* historical novel. "This book was begun on a safari in Africa and ended during a week-end visit in Long Island." It is possibly encouraging to learn that masterpieces do not spring from the heads of literary Joves, but it is agreeable once in a while to eat a dinner without being informed first that the cook has produced it at the cost of bankruptcy and complete exhaustion. It would be pleasant to read an effortless, flowing novel without being obliged to feel sorry for the author's effortful contrivance. Oddly enough, the books that an author tells us were a great trouble to write are sometimes, by a macabre coincidence, equally difficult to read. Homer managed to start his story without telling us of the warfare in his own breast; he had a war to tell about, and he lost no time in getting to it.

Forever Young

When the Guggenheim Foundation began awarding fellowships twenty-five years ago, they gave them to promising young men. There has been of late a change of policy, which change can be most dramatically realized when we find that the oldest recipient of a fellowship last year was a botanist seventy-six years of age. Two philosophers in their forties were granted awards, and there was a scattering of scholars and writers in their fifties and sixties. We have heard able people cogently deplore this granting of fellowships for scholarly and creative work to the middle-aged and the elderly. They say not only that youth should be given a chance, but they cite arguments to show that creativeness always ends, at the latest, in the early thirties—sometimes by death, as with Byron or Mozart.

Well, the new Guggenheim line will bring comfort to a great many of us whose opinions on these matters change a little as we grow older. Good old Guggenheims, remembering that middle age, too, has its talents, and that there are creative outbursts in old age! Someone must have reminded the Guggenheims that Verdi wrote *Falstaff* (which some think his greatest masterpiece) when he was eighty. Matthew Arnold did not really get going as a poet until late middle age. Alfred North Whitehead began his real career as a philosopher when he was sixty-five. Robert Frost as a poet does more than all right at seventy-five. And who ever thought the middle-aged and the old did not need freedom to work as much or more than the young? The young are often not yet embroiled in families or professions. They do not need a chance to get a second wind. The Guggenheims have a fine fresh notion: Age will be served. And heaven knows what may come of it! Older Guggenheim fellows have a particular responsibility to do well. They owe it to their senescing contemporaries who are waiting to apply next year. John Dewey, still an active thinker at ninety-one, is my candidate. A fellowship would be a great encouragement to him, and to a great many other people, too.

Not the Way I Remember It

If there had been survivors of the Flood beyond Noah's family, they would have been tempted in their later years to correct narratives of that inundating event as reconstructed by their juniors. "That," some graybeard must have remarked, "was not the way it happened; as far as I remember it, Noah was *not* drunk. It's curious the way these legends get started." Those of us whom *Time* Magazine would call "oldsters" or, perhaps, "middle-oldsters," who were young in the 'twenties, are beginning to read books written by young men who were tots in the 'twenties, and who now with industry and imagination "get up" the 'twenties and make that decade the theme of historical fiction or, perhaps, of semi-fictional history.

One tries to remember back to the days of the speakeasy, of the Charleston, of the Lindbergh flight, of the early Hemingway, of the American (peacetime) invasion of the Riviera, to the days of speculative fever when every elevator boy was buying stock on margin in a bullish economy that could never reach a final top. One tries to recall the jazz age and flaming youth; one remembers George Gershwin and Edna St. Vincent Millay.

Well, all of us who were young then remember even at that time *reading* about all these things. But, perversely, one seems to recall that a great deal of all this was very remote, at the time, to precisely the kind of young people who are reading about it now and believing that the more spectacular elements of the era completely characterized their predecessors. The mad 'twenties? How many of one's friends lived colorlessly sane lives! How few people some of us seem to have known who were speculating on the stock market; how relatively rare was a visit to a speakeasy! I once saw Texas Guinan plain, but that was because a visiting Frenchman insisted on going to a night club where he could see this American phenomenon. Texas Guinan gave me a rose; I wish I could regard it as the tenderest of my memories.

The life reported in *This Side of Paradise* was as frivolous and special to most young men and women of that period as it is today. A great many of us used to read with envy about flaming youth; it never occurred to us in dormitory rooms or library cubicles that *we* were *it*. How grand it is to discover now, belatedly, that the whole generation of young people in the 'twenties was glamorously unshackled, expensively sinful, spiritually lost in far and exotic places. Most of us, even when we went to Europe, were not part of any grand and tragic international set. We lived in *pensions* where we met elderly English spinsters, and some of the worst sins we committed were on French irregular verbs. Often we had breakfast, even lunch, in dairies, not even in cafés, and for some of us, at least, spiritual enrichment came from the works of Poincaré and Bergson, rather than Joyce and Lawrence.

What a pity we let the mad, bad, glad, sad, glamorous 'twenties slip through our fingers. How lucky for us that we have lived to read about them now.

On Keeping the Old Familiar Faces

If only the industrious scholars would quit for a while, then one could live among the comfortable, familiar legends of one's youth. There was a time when Plato seemed Platonic and Browning Browningesque. The Greeks were all white marble classicism, and Machiavelli Machiavellian. Alas, zealous research has upset all that. The Reformation was not quite the Reformation, and the Renaissance began earlier or later than one had supposed, or, perhaps, strictly speaking, not at all.

Except in the region of our own specialties, all of us live in a spiritual geography of cozy, established formulas, and one hates to see the old landmarks fade, or get defaced, or disappear altogether. Thus recently we have been given in a brilliant biography clear evidence of what we should earlier have suspected, that Florence Nightingale was neither the "lady with the lamp" of late Victorian sentiment, nor the exhibitionist of good works and dogmatic opinions she became for Lytton Strachey. It turns out that she was a complicated being worthy the reflections of an Ibsen or a Freud. Browning, in spite of all his ripe optimism and dashing chivalrous vigor, turns out from his private letters to have been brisk, business-like, sensible, and even irritable. Even the Plato of the eternal essences, the philosopher-king, has become much more complex, mathematical, semantic than Raphael or Ficino knew.

Yet many of us in our secret hearts, next to our newer,

borrowed knowledge, keep our earlier myths. A little learning is a winsome thing. It gives us the child Haydn, the Ariel Shelley, the lyric Joan of Arc. The new figures scholarship gives us cannot compare in simplicity, in human appeal, with these myths we have cherished so long. It is interesting to meet Florence Nightingale the great hospital administrator, the active lobbyist for good causes, the lady of a thousand suppressed passions. But she'll never quite oust from one's imagination the Lady with the Lamp.

Exchange of Opinion

Nothing, we have been told these many democratic years, is more educative than participating in or listening to an exchange of opinion. The colloquium, the seminar, the conference, the symposium, the panel discussion on the radio—how fine, how liberating, how instructive these are to us all, to the participants, to those in the gallery, to those at their receiving sets. The reputed values hardly need to be mentioned. Opinions we had long held are promptly modified; there are persuasively insinuated into our minds things we had never thought of up to that moment. Theories we had deemed incompatible are clearly synonymous. Why had it never occurred to us before that planned economy and free enterprise really go very well together? Why had we not realized that isolationists and internationalists are really saying one and the same thing? How stupid of us not to have comprehended that atheists and theists, socialists and capitalists, devotees of program music and of absolute music, vegetarians and beef-eaters, really have everything in common! In theory, at least, the chief value of a panel discussion is to help us see that intelligent men all agree on everything. All that is required is a skilled moderator to bring out this salubrious awareness.

How different in fact are the results of listening to or, even more, of participating in, such a discussion. After a half hour we *have* generally learned something, something wonderfully reviving too. It becomes perfectly clear that we were even more in the right than we had believed at the outset. How surprising to find that such intelligent colleagues can be so completely wrong-headed, even after the truth is made plain to them. It is gratifying to us to see that the only points, sharp, relevant and true, that were made were our own. And, as some friend, always happily present, points out to us, we were the only one who spoke complete, grammatical sentences, who kept his temper; it is we alone who showed an unwavering concern for justice and truth. One would hardly have believed, until one actually heard the others, that such absurd convictions, such ineptness in debate, such bad intellectual manners could exist among literate people. There is nothing quite like an exchange of opinions for an hour or so to convince one of the superiority of one's own opinions to the quite silly ideas other people so naïvely broach.

The Renascence of Sin

A conviction of sin, it is becoming fashionable again to assert, is the prerequisite to effective improvement in the world. The trouble with liberalism of the nineteenth-century variety, theologians enthusiastically advise us, is, or was, its smug optimism, its naïve faith in human nature, its bland assumption that we are, if not nature's masterpieces, at least nature's good boys. Just look at the history of the past forty years, we are told, and one will see the silliness of such assumptions. We are nature's bad boys, we are miserable sinners, we are vessels of corruption, we are bodies of this death. If only we had had the sense to read St. Paul more carefully, we should have known this all along—and we would know also from whom the new theologians are plagiarizing.

Hardly a man is now wickedly alive who could deny the monstrosities, the perversities, the cruelties, that our human nature has exhibited on a vast scale in these last decades. If it is not the psychiatrists, it is the theologians who remind us what depths unmentionable are in our natures. All this should, one supposes, have a tonic effect upon us. But it is clear to some of us, at least, that these home truths (and from what a reputable home!) about ourselves do not help us much. If human nature is the sink of iniquity happily claimed for it by the neo-St.-Pauls of our time, then, save for grace (which it is hard to believe will ever reach such as us), the world is really doomed. Is it rapscallions like us who are going to improve society, avert wars, sustain peace? Absurd. Is it we in our pride who are going to have the insolence to start fresh?

Well, if we cannot be washed clean, we may as well wallow in the dirt of our sins and enjoy our own nastiness. There is at least one comfort. Even the criers of "Unclean" are, by their own definitions, as unclean as ourselves. They can be holier than ourselves only by glorying in their own iniquities, and hence by that show of spiritual pride making it evident that in one respect at least they are even more sinful than we are. The old-fashioned liberal had a sense, at least, of some fundamental goodness in human nature, with which we could improve civilization. But one can't make bricks without straw, and, if no good can come from people like us, at least we can draw, sinful though it be, a sigh of relief. Who are we to set ourselves up to improve the world? The devil must smile as he watches us relax—under the guidance of theologians.

Reasons for Celebration

There are families one knows where the ordinary regular birthdays of the members are hardly adequate to the capacity for celebration latent in the lively household. It becomes family practice to celebrate half-birthdays. Thus it becomes possible to signalize on a green lawn in July the natal day of a child whose regular birthday occurs in the bleakness of January. What is more important, the number of occasions for jollity is doubled, and there are ten sound excuses for festival where, by a less creative calendar, there would be only five.

But birthdays are hardly necessary, and certainly there are other plausible excuses for turning what are otherwise mere dates into red-letter days. Somebody is always leaving for, or arriving from, somewhere, or getting promoted, or having a book—or even a book review—published. Some friend has found a new house, a new apartment, even a new room, a discovery these days surely a cause for cooperative jubilation. And so great is the need for gregarious cheer that the excuses multiply and the slimmest reason is soon stout enough. "So-and-so," we may soon be saying, "has an idea for a new book. Let's give him a party"—and during it we may even find him a title—or a subject. The Campbells' house has just been repainted. Jim's son has made the high-school chess team. Edward's sister has decided to take up painting. The least that is called for is cocktails and processed cheese.

One would think in these times, haunted by the scuttle

butt of doom, celebrations would seem out of order, and that even the impulse to have them would vanish. There are probably no statistics on the subject, but there is surely no harm in guessing what they would show. Statistics, then, if one had them, would show that there is a notable stepping-up in the celebrations per capita, and an equally notable diminution in the importance of the reasons for having festivals, giving parties, organizing little enterprises of shared enjoyment. There must have been agreeable little orgies going on at Pompeii the night before it was buried, possibly lasting into the very morning of destruction—though, presumably, the celebrants at Pompeii did not know this was the last party anybody was going to give in that region.

Our little festivals are given on the conscious edge of destruction. But after all, in an anxious time it is not surprising that we welcome any flimsy excuse to indulge in festivities. Or perhaps the persistence of these little gatherings at somebody's house is a sign of a deep confidence that, somehow, there *is* going to be a world in which the new house can be lived in, the new job can be grown into, the new honor can be enjoyed, the new baby can grow up. To the long perspective it may be *earlier* than we think, and even this little gleam of hope is worth celebrating. Let's, then, have a party, just a small one, pending the breaking out of world peace, when the celebration will be very large and crowded and, one suspects, will soon get quite out of bounds.

Conclusion

THESE meditations, these incidental causeries, might have gone on over a much longer period and thus have filled a much longer book. They were provoked often by specific occasions, some personal or trivial, some national or world-wide. Indeed, for the reflective mind it may be said that all occasions, even the most intimate ones, have their larger setting in the universal condition of man. Especially in our own day it becomes at times laughably, at times tragically, clear how much our private lives have become functions of public events and how we often secretly estimate public events by what they mean to us in our private lives.

In any case, even the most casual circumstance must suggest to a meditative intelligence something that outlasts the moment and something that preceded it. These little essays have been drawn from a period of seven years. A different seven years would have provided different incitements to the play of mind or fancy. In the now so calm-looking days of the first decade of the twentieth century there would have been other fading events to provoke one's analysis or one's commentary. In 1984 or 1994 there will again be other, perhaps unimaginable, events, in an era which presumably will be either calmer or more completely chaotic.

I cannot resist speculating on what I might have found to comment upon had I been writing these essays in

1905 or 1910. I have a feeling that I should have gently deplored the passing of the Welsbach gas mantle, still, as I dimly remember it from earliest childhood, the lovliest, softest light for reading ever made by the ingenuity of man. Fluorescent lighting seems to me a glaring outrage in comparison with it. Certainly the ordinary electric-light bulb belongs where it has become most celebrated, assailing the eyes of some political prisoner abused by an interrogator in a grim totalitarian prison. I have a suspicion that I should have bemoaned the passion for speed that was afflicting bicycle riders and that I should have sighed with relief, knowing that the small vogue of the "century," the cycling accomplishment of a hundred miles in a single day, had passed.

Sometime or other even my essentially non-political mind would have come around to some comment on the unprecedented corruption existing in municipal, state, and federal government. The relation of crime and politics would have seemed to me to be a sinister new thing in the world, but I should probably have cheerfully declared that this was a transient phenomenon of a transition period, and that by mid-century political honesty would be routine.

Nor can I refrain from trying to imagine what I would be prompted to muse upon in 1994. The world, I should doubtless be pointing out, is now too close together. Two hours between New York and London really removes spaciousness and diversity from the world. How much better, I should be saying, things were in 1950 when it took at least fourteen hours to get from New York to London. In two hours one scarcely has time to change one's mind, or one's accent.

But these lucubrations were written at this time. They reflect, to a certain extent and inevitably, the geographic and personal station of their writer, uneasy but somehow not entirely unhappy in our unstable society. In that sense these brief notations are quite accidental. But in another sense they are not accidents at all. There are recurrent temperaments in the world and recurrent human situations; else the literature of the past would be wholly unintelligible to us. "Please don't speak so roughly of Clytemnestra," a student said to a friend of mine. "She's just like my mother." Family life, even violent family life, is very much the same in all ages, and while the occasions for what I have said might have been different, I probably should have said the same things.

But perhaps in 1994 I should not be saying the same things, or, innocuous as these pages may have seemed to the reader, would I be allowed to say the same things. We are by all the signs moving into an era of standardization, of suffocating order, not altogether caused by external threats of tyranny. Soon play of mind and freedom of imagination may be completely suspect. The charge of triviality may come to be one of the most serious accusations one can make against a writer, or almost equally serious by 1994 may be the charge of inconclusiveness, of indefiniteness; and tolerance may come to be the sign not of a just but of an empty mind. Only such literary works may be permitted as teach a wholesome doctrine, such as equality or justice, dogmatically defined by government edict. Only such treatises may be permitted as communicate facts it is considered urgent and timely to know. The reflective essay may be forbidden by public opinion if not by law. The merely playful exercises of the mind or of memory or invention may be regarded as truancy from rational behavior. The book that is merely harmless may be judged by that time the most harmful of all.

This essay is headed "Conclusion" and should therefore conclude something. All the ideas broached should be gathered together in one architectonic summary. It should appear that all these variations are variations on a common theme, that they are expressions of a single and coherent point of view, that they constitute one cosmos, reveal one consistent mind, one unvarying temper. Or, at the very least, these pages should conclude on some high note, like that of a tenor who has saved up his energies for the purpose. Or there should at least be a dying fall, a soft breathing into silence.

I cannot pretend that I can point to a single, comprehensive master-motif, or that I can manage some high lyric note on which to end. Nor, despite the troubles of our era and the perpetual prospect of death which faces us all—the atomic bomb or not—do I feel it necessary to end on a dying fall.

Indeed, I propose to continue these reflections, and another day (for I exuberantly presume there will be some other day) to invite the friendly reader to consider some other occasions, and some fresh or perhaps identical morals, which I shall doubtless feel compelled to draw from them. This conclusion may therefore stop just about here—just as lives stop, which, save for the accidents of nature and society, might have gone on longer or might have stopped long ago. Moreover, this is, we are constantly reminded, a time of pressing urgency. I am sure the reader who has come thus far ought to return to his chores—as should I. We all live under the same sky, but we all live on the same earth, too, in which there are other things to be done than to read—or to write.